SkillsBook

Grade 4

GREAT SOURCE®

HOUGHTON MIFFLIN HARCOURT

A Few Words About the *Texas Write Source SkillsBook* Grade 4

Before you begin . . .

The *SkillsBook* provides you with opportunities to practice editing and proofreading skills presented in the Student Edition of *Texas Write Source* text. It contains guidelines, examples, and models to help you complete your work in the *SkillsBook*.

Each *SkillsBook* activity includes a brief introduction to the topic and examples showing how to complete that activity. You will be directed to the page numbers in the Student Edition of *Texas Write Source* textbook for additional information and examples. The "Proofreading Activities" focus on punctuation and the mechanics of writing, usage, and spelling. The "Sentence Activities" provide practice in sentence combining and in correcting common sentence problems. The "Language Activities" highlight the parts of speech.

The Next Step and Learning Language

Most activities include one of these two features at the end of the exercise. They provide ideas for follow-up work that applies what you have learned to your own writing and speaking.

Photo Acknowledgements Cover ©Brand X/Getty Images.

Printed in the U.S.A.

ISBN-13 978-0-547-39566-1

12 0928 19 18 17 16

4500584669 B C D E F G

Table of Contents

Proofreading Activities

Handwriting Practice

Editing for Mechanics

Improving Spelling

Using the Right Word

Sentence Activities

Sentence Basics

Sentence Problems

Sentence Combining

Sentence Variety

Language Activities

Nouns

Pronouns

Verbs

Adjectives

Adverbs

Prepositions

Conjunctions and Transitions

Interjections

Parts of Speech Review

Proofreading Activities

This book begins with handwriting instruction and practice. Then proofreading activities provide practice checking sentences for punctuation, mechanics, and usage. Most activities also include helpful references in the Student Edition of *Texas Write Source*. **The Next Step** and **Learning Language** activities encourage follow-up skills practice.

TEKS 4.21A

Manuscript Printing

Good handwriting is important. You have learned two kinds of handwriting: manuscript printing and cursive script. Use manuscript printing when you are filling out forms, when your lettering has to be especially neat (for example, on posters), or when your teacher asks you to use it.

Practice your manuscript printing. Trace the letters that you see on this page. Then copy them on the blank lines.

Aa Bb Cc Dd Ee Ff

Gg Hh Ii Jj Kk Ll

Mm Nn Oo Pp Qq Rr

Ss Tt Uu Vv Ww Xx

Yy Zz

TEKS 4.21A

The Next Step **On the lines below, copy a paragraph from an essay that you have already written. Use your best manuscript printing.**

Many printed capital letters are a mix of horizontal lines and vertical lines. Draw horizontal lines from left to right. Draw vertical lines from top to bottom.

TEKS 4.21A

Cursive Script

Good handwriting—whether it is manuscript printing or cursive script—shows that you care about your writing. Use cursive script when you are being formal (for example, with compositions and business letters) and when your teacher asks you to use it.

Practice your cursive script. Trace the letters that you see on this page. Then copy them on the blank lines.

Aa Bb Cc Dd Ee Ff

Gg Hh Ii Jj Kk

Ll Mm Nn Oo Pp

Qq Rr Ss Tt Uu

Vv Ww Xx Yy Zz

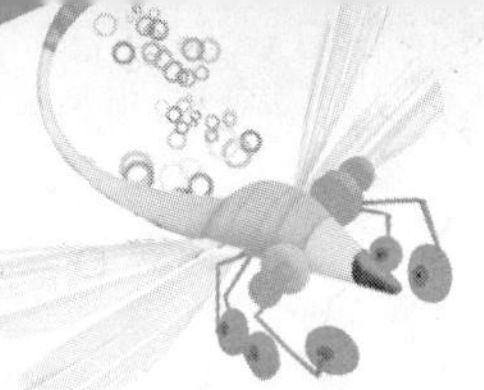

TEKS 4.21A

The Next Step Choose a short piece of writing from your writing folder. Copy it on the lines below, using your best cursive script.

Think about spacing as you write. Keep the same space between the letters in each word. Keep the same space between words, too.

End Punctuation 1

There are three ways to end a sentence. You may use a **period**, a **question mark**, or an **exclamation point**. (See *Write Source* pages 527 and 528.)

Examples

Animals *talk* in many ways.

Do you understand your dog's barking?

It's raining cats and dogs!

Put the correct end punctuation in the sentences below. You will also need to add a capital letter at the beginning of each sentence. The first sentence has been done for you.

Did you know that many animals have their own language? dolphins "talk" by making clicking sounds a dolphin can make as many as 700 clicks in one second bees "talk" by flying in patterns like dancing they tell other bees where to find flowers.

some animals even "speak" in ways that humans might understand have you ever noticed that dogs have different barks a dog barks one way when someone is at the door and another way when it is hurt

a gorilla named Koko has gone one step further she actually talks to humans she has learned a sign language when a kitten bit Koko, she made signs to say, "Teeth visit gorilla." it is not the way you would say it, but you know what she meant "Ouch"

ELPS 4C, 5G

End Punctuation 2

This page lets you practice using end punctuation. (See *Write Source* pages 527 and 528.)

Examples

Years ago, a cat named Napoleon became famous.

Do you know why?

He could predict the weather!

Put the correct end punctuation in the sentences below. You'll also need to add a capital letter at the beginning of each sentence. The first sentence has been done for you.

Napoleon lived in Baltimore with his owner. in the summer of 1930, it didn't rain for a long time one day, Napoleon's owner called the newspapers and said that rain was on the way they didn't believe him, but Napoleon's owner knew better Napoleon was napping with one front paw stretched out and his head on the floor whenever Napoleon did that, it soon began to rain

what do you think happened yes it poured and poured from then on, the newspapers printed Napoleon's weather forecasts he was right as often as the human weather forecaster don't you wish you had a cat like Napoleon at your house

The Next Step **People often ask questions and make comments about the weather. Write at least five sentences related to the weather. Be sure to use the correct end punctuation!**

ELPS 4C, 5G

Commas Between Items in a Series 1

Commas are used between words or phrases in a series. (See *Write Source* page 530.)

Example

I have pen pals in *Australia*, *Greece*, and *Ireland.*

In the paragraph below, add commas between items in a series. The first sentence has been done for you.

Antarctica, Europe, and Australia are continents. Australia is the only country that takes up a whole continent. Australia has many large deserts some coastal rain forests and the world's largest coral reef. The reef is called the Great Barrier Reef is 1,200 miles long and is on the northeast coast. Australia is surrounded by the Indian Ocean Coral Sea and Tasman Sea. Kangaroos kookaburras and dingoes are just a few of the unusual animals that live in Australia. Queensland Victoria and New South Wales are three of Australia's states. Queensland is the size of California Arizona New Mexico and Texas combined. Australia has diamonds gold copper and other gems and minerals.

The Next Step **Write four sentences of your own about Australia or another place. Use commas in a series in at least two of your sentences.**

ELPS 4C

Commas Between Items in a Series 2

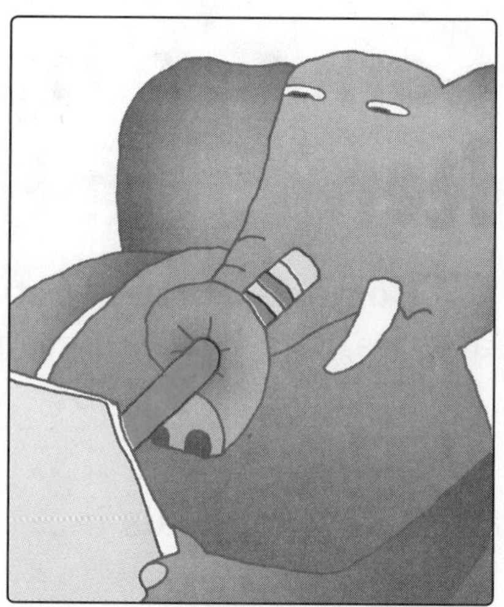

Commas are used between words or phrases in a series. (See *Write Source* page 530.)

Example

I have seen elephants *at zoos*, *at circuses*, and *at safari parks.*

In the sentences below, add commas between items in a series. The first sentence has been done for you.

Elephants are not just huge, heavy, and clumsy. They can do amazing things. Everyone knows that elephants use their trunks to hold things take up water and throw dust. Siri, a zoo elephant, held a rock in her trunk scratched it on the floor and drew designs. The zookeeper gave Siri a pencil and paper, and she kept drawing.

Elephants eat grass shrubs branches leaves bark roots and fruit. Sometimes they knock down trees rip off their bark and dig up their roots. Wild elephants eat 600–800 pounds of food a day.

Elephants' sharp tusks long trunks and crushing feet can be dangerous. Elephants also can be intelligent protective and gentle. Once a baby elephant got hurt. The herd followed the leader found a park ranger and led the ranger back to the baby elephant.

Commas in Compound Sentences

Commas are used between independent clauses that are joined by words such as *and, but, or, nor, for, so,* and *yet.* (See *Write Source* page 530.)

Example

Bats sleep all day, *but* they eat mosquitoes and other insects all night.

In the sentences below, add commas between the independent clauses in compound sentences. The first sentence has been done for you.

Hundreds of years ago, the United States was covered with forests, grassy fields, and deserts, so animals lived everywhere! Today there are more people and they have built homes and shops where animals used to live. Because of these changes, many animals left urban areas but some have adapted to cities.

If you have a cat, put a bell on its collar or it may sneak up on wild animals. Put water in a birdbath or other shallow container for birds. Plant a berry bush and it will provide food for wild animals. Buy a bat house at the hardware store and encourage this helpful insect eater.

The Next Step **Write a paragraph about things you can do to help animals in your neighborhood. Use compound sentences in your paragraph, and be sure to place to commas correctly.**

ELPS 4C, 5F

Commas to Set Off Introductory Phrases and Clauses

Commas can be used to set off long phrases and clauses that come before the main part of the sentence. (See *Write Source* page 532.)

Example

In the last few years, most cities have developed recycling programs.

Each sentence below starts with a long phrase or clause that modifies the rest of the sentence. Add a comma after each phrase or clause. The first sentence has been done for you.

1. If you want to help the environment, you can recycle many things.
2. Because glass never wears out it can be recycled forever.
3. Though it's hard to believe people have been recycling glass for more than 3,000 years!
4. At most recycling stations you'll find a bin for aluminum cans.
5. Even with all the different kinds most plastic can be recycled, too.
6. To recycle plastic you must separate the different kinds.
7. To avoid polluting the environment car oil is recycled.
8. Because there are many uses for tires people recycle them, also.

The Next Step **Write a letter to your school principal (or your city council) about recycling. Begin several sentences with long introductory phrases or clauses. Be sure to use commas correctly. (See the sample letter on *Write Source* page 240.)**

ELPS 4C

Commas in Dates and Addresses

Commas are used to set off the different parts in addresses and dates. (See *Write Source* page 532.)

Example

My best friend's address is 419 Royal Lane, Plano, Texas 75086. He moved here from Boston, Massachusetts, on August 4, 2009.

Add commas where they are needed in the addresses and dates below.

My sister and I wanted to go to a theme park for our vacation—maybe in Orlando Florida or around Los Angeles California. Instead we will go camping in one of our state parks. To start planning, we sent for information from the Texas Parks and Wildlife Department 4200 Smith School Road Austin Texas 78744 on January 28 2010. A large packet of information arrived on February 5 2010. After looking it over, Mom decided that we should camp in Palo Duro Canyon State Park near Amarillo Texas. She says that we will camp for a whole week starting on June 24 2010. That means we won't have to break camp until July 1 2010. We'll ride horses, hike, see the *TEXAS* musical play, and tell stories around the campfire. Some of the towns we'll drive through on our vacation are Bellevue Texas; Wichita Falls Texas; and Goodnight Texas. We can't wait to go!

ELPS 4C

Commas to Keep Numbers Clear

Commas are placed between hundreds, thousands, millions, and so on. (See *Write Source* page 532.)

Example

The planet Mercury is 36,000,000 miles from the sun.
(You may also write the number this way: 36 million.)

Directions ▶ **Add commas to numbers where they are needed in the sentences below.**

1. The surface of the sun is a sizzling 11000 degrees Fahrenheit.
2. The center of the sun burns even hotter at 27000000 degrees!
3. Even though it is 93000000 miles away from Earth, the sun can heat some places on our planet to around 136 degrees Fahrenheit.
4. Pluto takes 90520 days to revolve around the sun once. With a "year" that long, summer vacation would last 22630 days!
5. Because gravity is weak on Mars, a 2000-pound elephant would weigh only 760 pounds.
6. On Jupiter, because of strong gravity, the same elephant would weigh 5060 pounds.
7. Venus and Earth are about the same size. Earth's diameter is 7926 miles, and Venus's is 7519 miles.
8. Jupiter is the largest planet in our solar system with a humongous diameter of 88736 miles.

ELPS 4C

Commas to Set Off Interruptions

Commas are used to set off a word or a phrase that interrupts the main thought of a sentence. (See *Write Source* page 534.)

Example

Eurasian reindeer are small. The male, in fact, is only four feet high at the shoulder.

Directions **Insert commas as needed in the sentences below.**

1. Reindeer are indeed strong animals.
2. A reindeer can pull twice its own weight actually on a sled.
3. Moreover reindeer can carry heavy burdens and riders.
4. These deer have been very important to northern people. Until recently, Laplanders as a matter of fact depended completely on the reindeer for their livelihood.
5. Reindeer after all can provide meat, milk, clothing, and transportation.
6. Reindeer feed on various plants. For example they eat grasses in the summer and lichens in the winter.
7. North America has its own version of the reindeer, called caribou. Caribou however are larger than their Eurasian cousins.

ELPS 4C

Commas in Direct Address

Commas are used to separate the person being spoken to from the rest of the sentence. (See *Write Source* page 534.)

Example

"Alicia, if you could travel anywhere in the world, where would you go?"

Directions ▶ **Insert commas where needed in the following sentences.**

1. "I want to go to Mongolia Ms. Baines."
2. "No way Alicia," said Maxie.
3. "Yeah, Alicia come on. Where do you really want to go?" asked Larry.
4. "Class let Alicia tell us about her dream," said Ms. Baines.
5. "I read about an 18-day trip to Mongolia Ms. Baines."
6. "Larry you get to ride horses for nine of those days!"
7. "You camp along the way Maxie and you learn how people lived way back in the days of Genghis Khan."
8. "What else do you get to do Alicia?" asked Ms. Baines.
9. "You eventually meet the Reindeer People in a remote mountain valley Ms. Baines. They're a nomad group who herd reindeer."
10. "You sit around campfires Maxie and listen to stories and eat 'horhog,' whatever that is."
11. "Gosh, Alicia it was sounding good until that part," piped up Larry.

ELPS 4C

Commas to Set Off Appositives

Commas are also used to set off appositives. (See *Write Source* page 536.)

Example

Bamboo, *a tall grass*, is used to build houses.
(The appositive *a tall grass* renames *bamboo*.)

Add a comma before and after (if needed) each appositive in the sentences below. The first sentence has been done for you.

1. Hogans, houses made of logs and mud, are built by the Navajo.
2. Igloos shelters made of packed snow are used by the Inuit.
3. Tepees cone-shaped tents are made from buffalo skins.
4. A tepee can easily be moved on a travois a sledlike carrier.
5. Yurts large domed tents made of skins or felt are shaped like igloos.
6. Yurts are built by people in Mongolia an area in Asia.
7. A laavu a tent much like a tepee is a shelter used in Lapland.
8. Lapland an area in northern Europe is cold and snowy.
9. In Hong Kong, some people live on sampans small houseboats.
10. The bones of mammoths mammals that are now extinct were used to build houses in the Stone Age.

Add an appositive to each of the following sentences. Begin your appositive where you see the caret (∧). You may add any word or phrase you like, as long as it renames the noun that comes before it. Use commas correctly. The first one has been done for you.

1. Our teacher ∧ read a story aloud.

   Our teacher, Ms. Garrett, read a story aloud.

2. My favorite book ∧ was checked out of the library.

   ____

   ____

3. Our principal ∧ came to our class.

   ____

   ____

The Next Step **Now complete the sentences below by adding an appositive and other words. The first one has been done for you.**

1. My favorite place *, Florida, is where my grandparents live.*

2. Our school ____________________________________

   ____

3. Our science book ________________________________

   ____

4. My hometown ___________________________________

   ____

ELPS 4C

Commas in Letter Writing

Commas are placed after the greeting in a friendly letter and after the closing in all letters. (See *Write Source* page 536.)

Example

Dear Sarah,

I can't wait till your visit, can you? When does your train . . .

Your best friend,
Maria

Make the needed corrections in the following exercises. If commas are already used correctly, write "C" on the blank.

1. ____ Dear President Obama:
   It has come to my . . .
   Sincerely;
   Martin Baines

2. ____ Dear Grandma,
   Thanks for the . . .
   Love
   Susie

3. ____ Dear Mrs. Settler,
   I hope you . . .
   Sincerely,
   Susie

4. ____ Dear Marty!
   How are you? I . . .
   Friends,
   Buzzy

5. ____ Dear Director:
   I am a student . . .
   Yours truly,
   Sally Farthing

6. ____ Dear Pedro
   For the next . . .
   Your friend
   Patricia

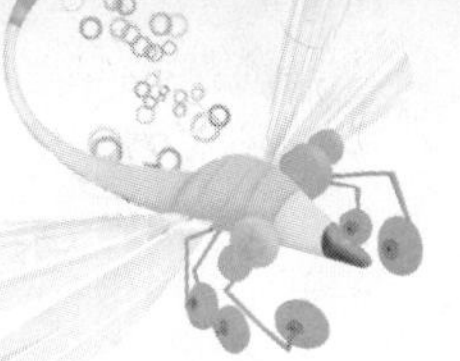

Commas Practice

Directions ▶ **Add commas correctly in the sentences below.**

“Yuri what did you decide to write about?”

“I didn’t decide yet Darius. How about you?”

“I picked a subject yesterday as a matter of fact. I read some magazines and I decided to write about climbing Mount Everest.”

Mount Everest the tallest mountain in the world is 29035 feet high. This majestic mountain is near Kathmandu Nepal on the Tibetan border. On May 29 1953 Edmund Hillary and Tenzing Norgay became the first climbers to reach the summit of Mount Everest. Norgay was a Sherpa a member of a Tibetan group who live in the high altitudes. They are expert mountain-climbing guides. Sherpas in fact helped the National Geographic 50th Anniversary Everest Expedition to the summit on May 25 2002. Although climbing the mountain was hard enough the group also made a documentary film along the way. You can write to the National Geographic Society 1145 17th Street N.W., Washington D.C. 20036, for more information about the expedition.

End Punctuation and Comma Review

Put commas and the correct end punctuation in the sentences below. Also capitalize the first letter of each sentence.

have you ever seen turtles the only reptiles with a shell in pet shops in the streets or on logs and rocks at the edge of a river or pond they were probably painted turtles or box turtles some cities and towns have crossing signs that warn drivers not to run over ducks geese or slow-moving turtles

there are many different kinds of turtles there are sea turtles desert turtles snapping turtles and others sea turtles are huge and they can live for 100 years in the United States desert tortoises live in the deserts of the Southwest these turtles could become extinct soon because cows are eating their homes they live under shrubs that cows like to eat can you guess how snapping turtles got their name when bothered they will try to bite anything that moves so watch out snapping turtles can weigh as much as 200 pounds some people like to make turtle soup using these fierce-looking turtles

The Next Step Turtles sometimes fall over on their backs when they try to climb up on something. They can't get right side up again unless someone helps them. Pretend that you're a turtle, and you're stuck on your back. Write a paragraph about how you feel before and after a human comes along and helps you back onto your feet. Be sure to use each of the three types of end punctuation at least once, and use commas where they are needed.

ELPS 4C, 5E, 5G

Apostrophes 1

Apostrophes are used in many different ways. One of the most common uses is making contractions. (See *Write Source* page 538.)

Example

You'd see penguins in Antarctica.
(You + would = You'd)

In the following sentences, make as many contractions as you can. The first contraction has been done for you. (The number of contractions you can make is indicated in parentheses.)

1. Antarctica is so frozen that people only visit; they ~~do not~~ don't live there. *(1)*
2. It is easy to get the Arctic and Antarctica mixed up. *(1)*
3. Here is a way to remember which is which. *(1)*
4. At the North Pole, the Arctic is an ocean that is surrounded by land. *(1)*
5. Antarctica is land that is surrounded by water, and it is at the South Pole. *(2)*
6. Polar bears and seals live on islands of ice in the Arctic, and they are at home there even though it is cold. *(2)*
7. Antarctica is even colder than the Arctic, but the penguins that live there do not seem to mind. *(1)*

The Next Step **Imagine that you went to Antarctica. Write a message to a friend telling her or him about your trip. Use as many contractions as you can.**

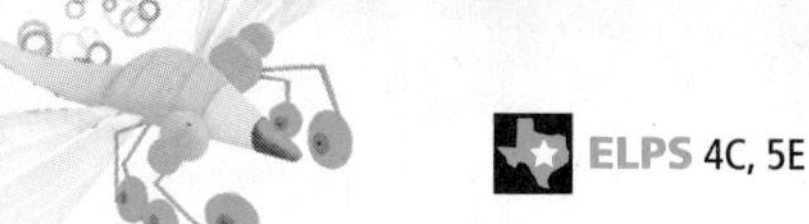

ELPS 4C, 5E

Apostrophes 2

Use an apostrophe and *s* to form the possessive of most singular nouns. Add just an apostrophe to make the possessive form of plural nouns ending in *s*. (See *Write Source* pages 538 and 540.)

Examples the dog's food an owner's manual the bees' buzzing

The possessive of a singular noun ending in an *s* or a *z* sound may be formed by adding just an apostrophe, unless it is a one-syllable word.

Examples Dickens' books (or) Dickens's books
Carlos' folder (or) Carlos's folder
James's hobby Mr. Jones's driveway

Write the correct possessive form above each underlined word in the sentences below.

1. The Arctic cold weather doesn't seem to bother the Inuit people.
2. Canada newest territory, Nunavut, is populated by the Inuit people.
3. Their ancestors way of life was based on fishing and hunting.
4. Inuit sled dogs played an important role in this people day-to-day life.
5. A sled dog strength is amazing, as he can pull one and a half times his own weight.
6. The dogs can sniff out a seal breathing hole for the hunters.
7. A sled dog bark is more like a wolf long, sad howl.
8. My dog, Sass, is much quieter than that, but Sass barking does upset my neighbor cat.

ELPS 4C, 5E

Apostrophes 3

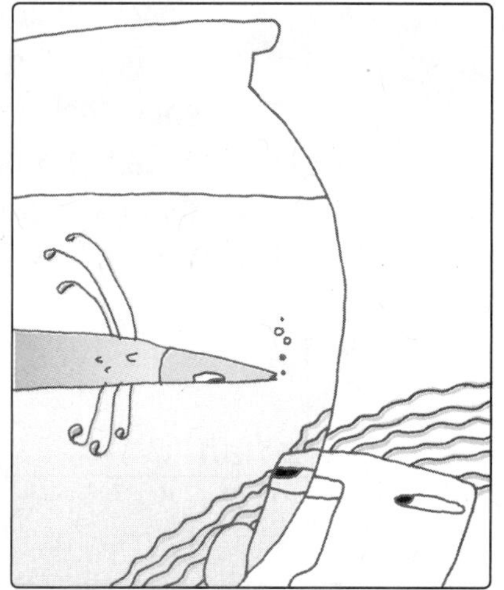

Apostrophes may be used to make possessives—to show ownership. (See *Write Source* pages 538 and 540.)

Example

I think *Mia's* pet is the most unusual one.
(The pet belongs to Mia.)

The *pets'* cages are colorful.
(The cages belong to the pets)

Each sentence below contains one or two possessive nouns that need an apostrophe (or an apostrophe *and* an *s*). Add what's needed to make the possessive form correct. The first sentence has been done for you.

1. Our teacher's husband is an airline pilot.
2. My oldest sisters puppy and my youngest brothers cat tease each other.
3. My fathers boss is from Singapore.
4. Aunt Doris hat flew out the window, and Moms scarf followed it.
5. Uncle Ross laughter could be heard around the block.
6. The bus tires ran over the hat and squashed it.
7. The boys soccer team played the girls soccer team.
8. At the zoo, the elephants cages are huge.
9. The snakes cages are made of glass.
10. All of my classmates art projects are on display.

ELPS 4C, 5E

Under "Singular Possessives," write down the names of four people you know. Imagine that each person has caught a fish. Using apostrophes correctly, show that each person owns a fish. Next, think of four pairs of people, and write them under "Plural Possessives." Use apostrophes correctly to show that each pair owns a fish. The first one in each category has been done for you.

Singular Possessives

1. *Joe's fish* __________
2. __________
3. __________
4. __________
5. __________

Plural Possessives

1. *Joe and Rosa's fish* __________
2. __________
3. __________
4. __________
5. __________

The Next Step **Write a short paragraph in which you use one of your singular possessives and one of your plural possessives from above.**

____

____

____

TEKS 4.21C(ii)
ELPS 4C, 5G

Quotation Marks 1

Use **quotation marks** before and after spoken words. Also use them with words taken directly from a piece of writing. (See *Write Source* page 542.)

Examples

"Rise and shine!" called Mom. The brochure told us that Wyoming has "fishing galore, gorgeous autumn color in the mountains, and breathtaking hiking trails."

Directions **Place quotation marks correctly in the following sentences.**

1. I'm very sure that the sun isn't up yet, yawned Bobbie.
2. But we are, said Grandpa. Come on! The fish are waiting.
3. The park newspaper has lots of advice. One paragraph starts out, Never leave food open in the campsite overnight.
4. Raccoons and bears can open coolers. Did you know that? asked Midge.
5. I don't want to see that happen! piped up Bobbie.
6. I think raccoons are cute, said Minnie.
7. Not when they're stealing your food, they're not, said Todd.
8. You're making me hungry, barked Grandpa. Let's catch some fish!
9. If the campers catch no fish, the park newspaper has another tip: Visit our dining lodge for good home cooking.

The Next Step **Write a short paragraph about people visiting a park. Include the people's dialogue about what they see. Be sure to use quotation marks correctly.**

Quotation Marks 2

Place **quotation marks** around titles of songs, poems, short stories, book chapters, and articles. (See *Write Source* 542.)

Examples

"My Old Kentucky Home" *(song)*
"Girl Finds Lost Treasure" *(article)*
"The Last Chance" *(book chapter)*
"That New Kid" *(short story)*
"Teeny Tiny Mice" *(poem)*

Insert quotation marks correctly in the following sentences. (Commas and periods go inside quotation marks.)

1. Sarah got scared reading the short story Ghosts in the Doghouse.
2. That magazine article about riding horses, Saddle Up for Adventure, sounds interesting to me.
3. Marcia loves horses, and she wrote two poems about them today: My Own Horse and Appaloosa Wind.
4. Reggie asked Mom to read two chapters of the book to him: Old Friends and Lifesavers.
5. The headline story in the school newspaper was No New Playground.
6. Casey taught us two songs: On Top of Old Smokey and The Honey Bee.
7. This morning's paper has an article about stray pets: Humane Society Shelter Overcrowded.

The Next Step **Write a short paragraph to describe a few of your favorite songs, stories, poems, or articles. Include the titles and punctuate them correctly.**

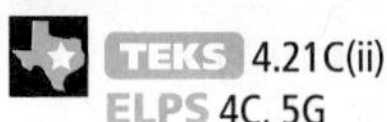
TEKS 4.21C(ii)
ELPS 4C, 5G

Punctuating Dialogue 1

When you talk, it's easy to tell who is saying what. However, when you write, you have to show when people start talking and when they stop talking. That's what **quotation marks** do. They come before and after the exact words someone says. (See *Write Source* page 542.)

Example

The bandleader said, "Let's have a zoo concert."

A band played a concert for some monkeys. A reporter interviewed the zookeeper about the concert. Add quotation marks where they should go. The first sentence has been done for you.

"Why would a band play for monkeys?" the reporter asked.

They wanted to see what the monkeys would do, answered the zookeeper.

Well, did the monkeys like the music? asked the reporter.

They couldn't stand it, the zookeeper said. One brave chimp tried to take away the bandleader's trombone to make him stop!

Did he stop? asked the reporter.

Yes, the zookeeper said. The band changed to a slow, quiet song, and the monkeys sat down.

The Next Step **Write a conversation that might take place after a concert at your school. Use quotation marks to help the reader understand when someone is speaking.**

TEKS 4.21C(ii)
ELPS 4C, 5G

Punctuating Dialogue 2

Practice using **quotation marks** to punctuate direct quotations. (See *Write Source* page 542.)

Example

“Today is recycling day!” I said.

Correctly punctuate the dialogue in the following sentences. The first sentence has been done for you.

“Did you put out the recycling bins?” Bill asked his sister.

No, Margaret answered. I thought you did.

Me? I did it the last time, Bill said.

Uh-uh! I did it the last time! Margaret insisted.

Mom said, Why don’t you both do it?

Good idea, said Bill as he gathered up the old newspapers.

Okay. I’ll get the plastic and glass, Margaret said. But we still have one problem.

What’s the problem? Bill asked.

Whose turn will it be next week? Margaret asked.

The Next Step **Continue the story, as Margaret and Bill get the grass clippings bagged for recycling. Write at least four sentences and use quotation marks and commas correctly. Start a new paragraph for each new speaker.**

Hyphens 1

Certain compound words are *always* hyphenated (*off-season* and *off-limits*). Other compound words are written as one word (*offspring* and *offbeat*). In other cases, **hyphens** are used to create single-thought adjectives (*off-and-on* friendship and *off-and-running* start). Hyphens sometimes join a letter to a word.

Example

Randi got a *red-and-white* striped scarf.

He made a *U-turn* with his snowmobile.

Replace the underlined adjectives with single-thought adjectives from the list to complete the following story. The first one has been done for you.

below-zero	face-to-the-wind	H-shaped	sound-swallowing
bone-chilling	A-frame	never-ending	steam-engine
cattle-herding	T-shirts	rodeo-like	storm-weary

bone-chilling

1. Despite the cold blizzard, today we're moving the cattle up north.
2. We all wore thermal clothes under our sweaters and jackets.
3. Now, instead of a fun ride, this would be windy, cold work.
4. The barks of the working dogs were lost in the roaring wind.
5. Later, the dogs would return to snug tentlike doghouses.
6. The very cold windchill left riders with fingers growing numb.
7. Steamy snorts rose above the heads of the cattle.
8. The rolling North Dakota prairie disappeared into endless white.
9. Finally, the outlines of the familiar barns appeared in the distance.
10. Tired riders could now turn their backs to the wind and head for home.

Hyphens 2

Hyphens are used to divide words at the end of a line and to form new words with the prefixes *all-*, *ex-*, *great-*, and *self-*. (See *Write Source* page 544.)

Example

Mom baked some hot, buttery **home-made** biscuits with **all-purpose** flour.

Review the rules in *Write Source* about dividing words. Then read the sentences below. If the word at the end of the line is divided correctly, write "C" on the short line. If not, show the correct way to divide or write the word.

___ Emma and I always wash the supper dishes by hand. The autom-

___ atic dishwasher has a broken switch. That seems old-

___ fashioned, but the dishes get clean, and Dad noticed that we do-

___ n't use as much electricity that way. Mom, too, is happy about be-

___ ing earth-friendly. She says the environment needs a few good fri-

___ ends. And do you think we would ever use a garbage dis-

___ posal? No way. Food garbage goes in the compost heap in the ba-

___ ckyard. It makes good fertilizer. All the rabbits in the neighborhood a-

___ gree that we have very tasty homegrown vegetables!

The Next Step **Combine the following prefixes and words, using hyphens correctly. Finally, write a sentence on your own paper using two of the words you created.**

ex (plus)	**self (plus)**	**all (plus)**
classmate ______________	winding ______________	star ______________
president ______________	cleaning ______________	around ______________

ELPS 4C

Colons 1

A **colon** is used to introduce a list in a sentence. (See *Write Source* page 546.)

Example

Each student could choose to make a model of one of the following: an adobe house, a tepee, a log cabin, or an igloo.

Add a colon where one is needed in each sentence below. The first sentence has been done for you.

1. Each model must have these parts: a door or an entrance, one opening to let light in, and one opening to let smoke out.
2. For my igloo, I need these materials a cookie sheet, sugar cubes, and frosting.
3. These three students are making adobe houses Marcia, Jamila, and Josh.
4. Real adobe is made from two ingredients mud and straw.
5. To make a model tepee, you could use the following leather, waxed paper, or felt.
6. A log cabin could be made from these materials rolled-up construction-paper logs, bread-dough logs, or real sticks.

The Next Step **Write two questions that call for lists. Then write a sentence to answer each question. Be sure to use a colon in each answer.**

Colons 2

Colons are used after the greeting in a business letter. (See *Write Source* page 546.)

Example

Dear Mr. and Mrs. Zinnen:

Our school has chosen you as honorary . . .

Sincerely,
Martha Ludding

Directions Write the correct greeting for a business letter to each of the people listed below.

Museum Director   Mr. Garganzola   Ms. Templeton
Dr. O'Leary   Professor Mann   Mrs. Rumsfeld

1. ____________________
2. ____________________
3. ____________________
4. ____________________
5. ____________________
6. ____________________

Directions Correct the punctuation in the following parts of business letters. Write "C" on the line if everything is correct.

1. ____ Dear Professor Mann;
   I am studying moths in our . . .
   Sincerely,
   Rob Starling

2. ____ Dear Park Ranger,
   Last year my family . . .
   Yours truly,
   Sarah Fast

3. ____ Dear Ms. Cannon:
   I want to do a report on . . .
   Sincerely,
   Bob Lane

4. ____ Dear Sergeant Keats!
   My brother is in your . . .
   Sincerely,
   Maria Reyez

ELPS 4C, 5F

Semicolons

A **semicolon** can be used, instead of a comma and a coordinating conjunction, to connect two independent clauses. (See *Write Source* page 548.)

Example

It was supposed to snow today, *but* it didn't.

It was supposed to snow today; it didn't.

In each sentence below, replace the comma and coordinating conjunction with a semicolon. The first sentence has been done for you.

1. A few minutes ago, the sun was shining, ~~yet~~ now it's raining!
2. Todd is all wet, and Terry is, too.
3. They got caught in the rain, but I didn't.
4. They were walking home from school, and the rain started.
5. They were near my house, so they ran for our door.
6. I got home early, so I escaped the rain.
7. They're staying here, and we're doing our homework together.
8. They needed to dry off first, though, for they were getting cold.
9. I gave Todd and Terry some dry clothes, but they didn't fit.
10. They called their mom, and she brought them some clothes.

The Next Step **Write three sentences that use a comma and a coordinating conjunction to connect two independent clauses. (See *Write Source* page 634 for a list of coordinating conjunctions.) Trade papers with a partner. Rewrite each other's sentences, using a semicolon instead of the comma and conjunction.**

Italics and Underlining

Italics, *a slanted type*, is used for certain titles and special words. You may also **underline** instead of using italic type. (See *Write Source* page 550.)

Examples

Oliver Twist *(book)*
Celtic Highlands *(CD)*
Edmund Fitzgerald *(ship)*
New York Times *(newspaper)*
Ice Age *(movie)*
Romeo and Juliet *(play)*
Air Force One *(presidential plane)*
Big Fish *(DVD)*
Tyrannosaurus rex *(scientific name)*
This Old House *(TV program)*
bonjour *(non-English word)*
Zoobooks *(magazine)*

Correctly underline titles and special words in the sentences below. Remember, not all titles should be underlined.

1. My dog-loving brother read the book Shiloh by Phyllis Reynolds Naylor.
2. I read One-Eyed Cat by Paula Fox for my book review assignment.
3. "Pirates at Their Own Funeral" is the name of a chapter in Mark Twain's The Adventures of Tom Sawyer.
4. Jake asked for the DVD How to Ride a Bike for his birthday.
5. The spaceship Apollo 13 was launched on April 11, 1970.
6. Grandma says she read about it in the Houston Chronicle newspaper.
7. The movie Apollo 13 with Tom Hanks was very popular.
8. Charles Lindbergh flew to Paris in the Spirit of Saint Louis in 1927.
9. The scientific name for the common grass snake is Natrix natrix.
10. I think I read that in the National Geographic magazine.

4.21C(ii)
ELPS 4C

Italics and Quotation Marks

Italics and **quotation marks** are used to punctuate titles. (See *Write Source* pages 542 and 550.)

Examples

I titled my poem "Singing Seashells."

Add the correct punctuation to the titles in the following sentences. Use underlining in place of italics. The first sentence has been done for you.

1. One chapter in Write Source is called "One Writer's Process."
2. On page 285 there is a tall tale called Pecos Bill Rides a Twister.
3. I like the haiku Summer on page 304 in Write Source.
4. The chapter Poems has a split couplet called Moira.
5. My favorite story is A Grand-Slam Day on pages 75–76.
6. Owl and Highlights for Children are two magazines that publish student writing.
7. For fun, I read to my family out of my Guinness Book of World Records.
8. Our community newspaper is the Standard Press.

TEKS 4.21C(ii)
ELPS 4C

Fill in each blank below with an example title. If you don't know a title for each category, look for one.

1. Title of a magazine: ____________________
2. Title of a magazine article: ____________________
3. Title of a movie: ____________________
4. Title of a DVD: ____________________
5. Title of a book: ____________________
6. Title of a poem: ____________________
7. Title of a TV show: ____________________
8. Title of a music CD: ____________________

The Next Step **Now write a paragraph using the titles you wrote down. (You may use more than one title in a sentence.) Make sure to punctuate the titles correctly.**

____

____

____

____

____

____

____

____

ELPS 4C, 5F

Dashes

A **dash** is used to show a sudden change in thought or direction. (See *Write Source* page 552.)

Example

Harriet the Spy—it was made into a movie—is by Louise Fitzhugh.

Directions

Each sentence below contains a sudden change in direction. Add dashes to show where each change begins and ends. The first sentence has been done for you.

1. Mildred D. Taylor — she wrote *Song of the Trees* — is my favorite author.
2. *Charlotte's Web* Charlotte is a spider is by E. B. White.
3. Molly's favorite story also about a spider is the one about Anansi.
4. *Little House on the Prairie* there was a TV show based on it is by Laura Ingalls Wilder.
5. *How to Eat Fried Worms* the whole book is as funny as the title is one of my favorites.
6. Yoshiko Uchida maybe you have read some of her books is a Japanese American.

The Next Step **Write two sentences about books, stories, or authors. Include a sudden change in direction in each sentence. Make sure to use dashes correctly.**

Parentheses

Parentheses are used around words that add extra information to a sentence or make an idea clearer. (See *Write Source* page 552.)

Example

The man in the white lab coat (Dr. Zimmerman) will conduct an experiment for the class.

Place parentheses around the phrases below that either add information or make an idea clearer.

Grandpa went to grade school another name for elementary school in the '50s. He remembers watching Mr. Wizard a science teacher every week on TV. Mr. Wizard did some experiments that explained information scientific principles in a fun way. Mr. Wizard taught a lesson about vacuums not the kind that clean carpets with a milk bottle, a candle, and a hard-boiled egg. Burning the candle in the bottle an old-fashioned glass kind used up the air, and then the egg balanced on top got pulled into the bottle. Vacuums empty spaces just naturally want to be filled with something. We learned in our science class that black holes outer-space vacuums pull matter into themselves with great force. Besides vacuums, Grandpa learned about electricity, magnets, and the effects of liquid nitrogen a very cold substance on rubber bands.

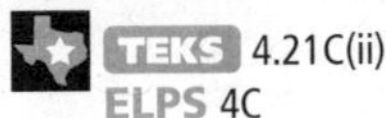
TEKS 4.21C(ii)
ELPS 4C

Punctuation Review 1

Add commas, quotation marks, and apostrophes where they are needed in the following sentences. The first sentence has been done for you.

1. Mom didn't believe me when I told her that Robby has five guinea pigs, three hamsters, three cats, two rabbits, and a goose.
2. Robby was kidding you she said. Or maybe you didnt hear what he said.
3. Being very curious my mom went over to Robbys house and she saw that I was right.
4. Five guinea pigs three hamsters three cats two rabbits and a goose! she said, shaking her head. I saw it and I still couldnt believe it!
5. Robbys mom Mrs. Davison explained that their family adopts animals that need homes.
6. The guinea pigs pen and hamsters cages are in Robbys room.
7. The cats favorite place is the kitchen.
8. The rabbits hutch is in the backyard.
9. The goose Buster lives in a big cage that Mr. Davison built.
10. Dear you know of course we cant have a zoo at our house Mom warned.

Add any needed punctuation to the sentence beginnings below. Then use your imagination, and correct punctuation, to complete the sentences and the story.

1. Robbys guinea pigs are named ______________________________

____

2. His hamsters names are ______________________________

____

3. The cats names are ______________________________

____

4. The rabbits names are ______________________________

____

5. Busters cage door was left open one day and a goose on the loose can

____

____

____

____

____

____

____

____

____

Punctuation Review 2

Each sentence below needs a semicolon or colon. Add the correct punctuation mark in the correct place.

1. Yesterday, our class had Ethnic Food Day everybody brought special snacks.
2. We sampled food from four continents Asia, Africa, Europe, and North America.
3. Sue's family is from Thailand she made watermelon slushes.
4. These are the ingredients for one watermelon slush three or four ice cubes, one cup of watermelon chunks, and one or two spoonfuls of sugar.
5. First you blend the ice cubes in a blender then you add the melon and sugar.
6. Blend again until everything is mixed your tropical treat is ready!
7. You can also use any of the following fruits pineapple, oranges, lemons, or limes.
8. Vijay said kids in India love popcorn they put red pepper on it instead of salt.
9. He said that kids in Nepal eat popcorn, too they put sugar on theirs!

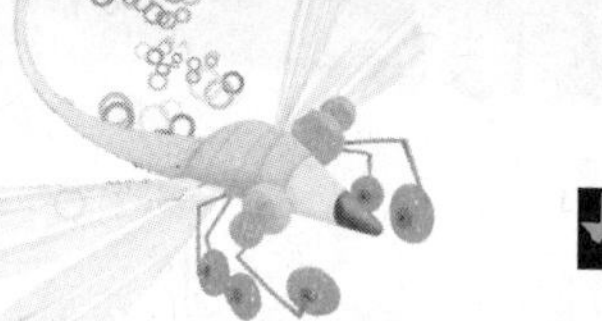

ELPS 4C

Directions **Add dashes or a hyphen to each sentence below. If a word is incorrectly divided at the end of a line, correct it.**

1. Hazelnut spread it's made with chocolate is a favorite snack in
   Europe.
2. Kids there especially in France eat hazelnut chocolate spread on bread after school.
3. Brian said chocolate sandwiches sounded like a half baked idea.
4. But Chantal she's from Paris got him to try some.
5. He said it was okay, but not his all time favorite.
6. "I'll stick with all American peanut butter and jelly," he said.
7. Chantal's dad is an ex chef.
8. He made a French snack using his great grandmother's recipe.
9. There were plenty of escargots that's French for snails for everyone.
10. Brian he's always trying to be funny said he wouldn't eat snails,
    even if they were dipped in hazelnut chocolate spread.
11. Peanut butter is a tasty, protein rich snack.
12. In Ghana that's a country in Africa people make peanut bu-
    tter soup.

ELPS 4C

Mixed Punctuation Review 1

This activity uses punctuation that you've seen in previous exercises. Get ready for a challenge! It includes dashes, end punctuation, italics and underlining, hyphens, colons, quotation marks, commas, and apostrophes.

Some of the punctuation has been left out of the following paragraphs. The number at the end of each line tells you how many punctuation marks need to be added to that line. Add the correct punctuation. The first line has been done for you.

1 My brother—he's in sixth grade—and I never agree on (2)
2 what videos to rent Last week, Peter that's my brothers (3)
3 name wanted Spider Boy II. I wanted Danger Dog: (3)
4 Revenge of the Monsters. Finally, we agreed to get Beauty (2)
5 and the Beast. We had both read the book and we wanted to (2)
6 see if the movie was as good. What do you think we found (1)
7 All the copies of course had been rented. (2)
8 "Now what?" my brother asked (1)
9 I guess we get our all time favorites again I said. (4)
10 We finally left the video store with the following movies (1)
11 A Fish Tale Star Adventures, Part 2 and Great Heart (6)
12 When our mom saw us she asked us why we didnt get (2)
13 something we hadnt seen before. Peter and I both said, (1)
14 "Dont ask!" (1)

ELPS 4C

Mixed Punctuation Review 2

This activity reviews seven kinds of punctuation.

Directions ▶ **Add the needed punctuation to the sentences below.**

Although many people dont know it Washington is the fourth capital of the United States Three other cities have served as the nations capital Philadelphia New York and Princeton The current capital is named for George Washington and he picked the diamond shaped site for the 100 square mile city The White House Congress and the Supreme Court are all in Washington DC

The White House home of the presidents family hasnt always been white In 1814, British soldiers burned it the house was left blackened by smoke After workers painted the house to cover the smoke it was called the White House President Andrew Jackson his nickname was Old Hickory added indoor plumbing

The White House has 132 rooms. The first floor rooms are used for public events These famous rooms include the East Room the Red Room the Green Room and the Blue Room Second floor and third floor rooms are where the First Family lives The White House has its own movie theater barbershop and dentists office

ELPS 4C

Capitalization 1

The basic rules for using **capital letters** are simple: Capitalize the first letter of a sentence and all proper nouns. Names of days, months, holidays, teams and their members, geographic places, and words used as names are all considered to be proper nouns. (See the rules on *Write Source* pages 554–560.)

Example

It was a *Saturday* baseball game in *July*.
(Capitalize the first letter of a sentence and all proper nouns.)

In the sentences below, find and change the words that should be capitalized. The first sentence has been done for you.

1. My uncle took my brother and me to see the south lake cardinals. (S L C)
2. The game was at birch stadium in south lake.
3. The cardinals played the chester rams.
4. My uncle said there was another game on sunday.
5. My brother said he didn't think mother would let us go; she wanted us to go with her to springfield, illinois.
6. But I said that maybe uncle could get mom to let us go to the game instead.
7. Then our uncle said he'd invite mom and dad to the game, too.
8. We all had a great time, and the cardinals won 10–7.

ELPS 4C

Directions **Capitalize words correctly in the following sentences.**

1. On the fourth of july, we watched fireworks explode over lake michigan in milwaukee, wisconsin.
2. Earlier in the week, we saw the bingley circus at millburn park, which is built on the site of the old middleton county fairgrounds.
3. Our uncle still wanted to show us the milwaukee public museum and mitchell park horticultural conservatory.
4. We only had two days of our vacation left, thursday and friday, before we had to board a plane at general mitchell international airport and fly home to tampa, florida.
5. Next year, our relatives will visit florida in either november or december for thanksgiving or christmas.
6. We want to take them to lake okeechobee and to everglades national park.

The Next Step **Write a paragraph about a game, concert, or other event you attended or would like to attend. Include as much information as you can about when and where it was, what teams or performers you saw or would like to see, and so on. Be sure to capitalize correctly.**

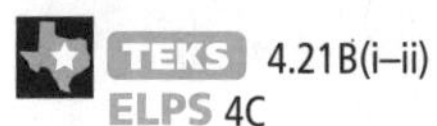

4.21B(i–ii)
ELPS 4C

Capitalization 3

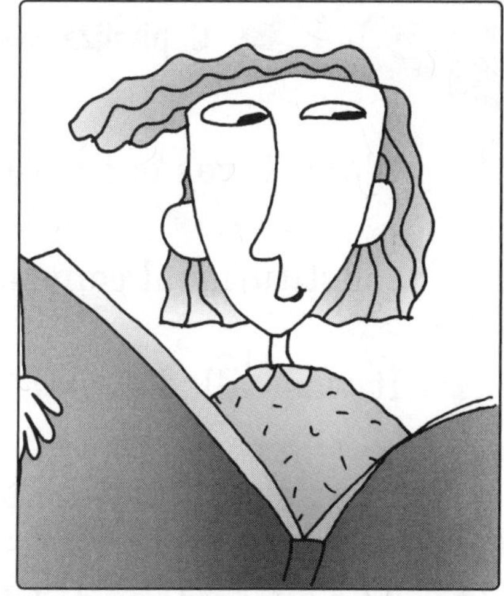

Capitalize the names of historical events and documents. Also capitalize titles of books, stories, and essays. Finally, capitalize the names of sections of the country, proper adjectives formed from such names, and the first word in a direct quotation. (See *Write Source* pages 558 and 560.)

Example

The book **Gone with the Wind** takes place in the **South** during the **Civil War**.

(Capitalize the title of a book, a section of the country, and an historical event.)

In the sentences below, find and change the words that should be capitalized. The first sentence has been done for you.

1. The war began 85 years after the declaration of independence was written and 78 years after the end of the american revolution

2. One famous book about that time is battle cry of freedom

3. My new story, “the conductors,” is about an event before the war.

4. Despite the fugitive slave act, the underground railroad kept leading enslaved people to freedom.

5. Abraham Lincoln signed the emancipation proclamation in 1863, on the same day as the battle of galveston.

6. The essay “remember the fallen” says that only world war II had more battlefield deaths than the civil war did.

Directions **Capitalize words correctly in the following sentences.**

1. When I was out west last summer, I read a novel about the constitutional convention.
2. It was called *summer in philadelphia*, and I told Marta about it.
3. She asked, "did the story take place before the war of 1812?"
4. "yes," I explained. "after the revolutionary war, the articles of confederation was the guide for our new government."
5. "it wasn't working well, so representatives from the north and the south went to Philadelphia in 1787."
6. Marta said, "i know that some of them had signed the declaration of independence, at the continental congress."
7. I went on, "they looked to the magna carta for ideas. They argued, too, over ideas like the virginia plan before creating the constitution."
8. Later, I wrote an essay called "a change in america's government." At the end, I wrote, "despite times of trouble, like the great depression and the vietnam war, the constitution still works."

The Next Step **Write five sentences about historical events that you might read about in stories and books. Be sure to capitalize correctly.**

TEKS 4.20A(ii)
ELPS 2C, 4C

Plurals 1

Singular nouns refer to one person, place, or thing. Plural nouns refer to more than one. There are many rules for making **plurals**. (See *Write Source* pages 562 and 564.)

Examples

cow ➜ cows
(Most nouns add an *-s.*)

church ➜ churches
(Nouns ending in *sh, ch, x, s,* or *z* add *-es.*)

penny ➜ pennies
(Nouns ending in *y* that follows a consonant change *y* to *i* and add *-es.*)

Directions ➜ **Write the plural form of each singular word listed below.**

1. fox ______________
2. beach ______________
3. class ______________
4. horse ______________
5. llama ______________
6. ash ______________
7. address ______________
8. tree ______________
9. lunch ______________
10. loss ______________
11. spider ______________
12. pony ______________
13. fly ______________
14. city ______________
15. bush ______________
16. day ______________
17. eye ______________
18. nest ______________
19. book ______________
20. boy ______________

Examples

radio ➜ **radios**
(Nouns ending in a vowel and *o* add *-s*.)

potato ➜ **potatoes**
(Nouns with a consonant before the *o* add *-es*.)

piano ➜ **pianos** alto ➜ **altos** taco ➜ **tacos**
(Musical and Spanish nouns ending in *o* add *-s*.)

handful ➜ **handfuls**
(Nouns ending in *ful* add *-s*.)

reef ➜ **reefs**
(Add *-s* if a final *f* is still heard in the plural form.)

knife ➜ **knives** hoof ➜ **hooves**
(Change *f* or *fe* to *v* and add *-es* when the plural form has a *v* sound.)

Directions ▶ **Underline the correct plural word within each set of parentheses.**

It was a normal day on the farm. My two aunts came from the garden with *(apronsfull / apronfuls)* of ripe *(tomatos / tomatoes)*. Farmers' *(wives / wifes)* are always busy. Uncle Fred was fixing the shed *(rooves / roofs)*. Grandpa and my brother were spreading straw for the *(calfs / calves)*. After our meal at the end of the day, which included *(loaves / loafs)* of homemade bread and jam, Grandpa brought out his *(banjoes / banjos)*. We had some music and *(soloes / solos)* besides the sing-alongs. Finally, Uncle Fred told the stories we'd all waited for—the ones about the *(rodeos / rodeoes)* he'd ridden in.

Learning Language **On your own paper, write a short story (real or made-up). Use as many of the singular and plural nouns on this and the previous page as you can. Then tell a partner a new sentence that uses singular and plural nouns.**

TEKS 4.20A(ii)
ELPS 2C, 2H, 3G, 4C, 5G

Plurals 2

Making plurals isn't always as simple as adding an *-s* or *-es* to the end of a word. Some nouns are irregular, and their spelling changes for the plural. Compound nouns add *-s* or *-es* to the main word. (See *Write Source* page 564.)

Examples

two men (irregular)

maids of honor in weddings (compound)

Directions ▶ **Make all of the following words plural. The first one has been done for you.**

1. woman *women*
2. child ____________
3. fish ____________
4. goose ____________
5. cactus ____________
6. ox ____________
7. tooth ____________
8. foot ____________
9. deer ____________
10. matron of honor ____________
11. brother-in-law ____________
12. secretary of state ____________
13. sheep ____________
14. mouse ____________
15. house of assembly ____________
16. father-in-law ____________
17. chief executive officer ____________
18. commander in chief ____________

Learning Language **On your own paper, write a paragraph about your family that uses irregular plural nouns. Then tell a partner a new sentence that uses irregular plural nouns.**

Plurals Review

Working in groups, think of a noun that fits each of the plural rules in your text. Write down at least one word for each rule; then write its plural form.

1. *Singular noun:* ____________________

   Plural noun: ____________________

2. *Singular noun:* ____________________

   Plural noun: ____________________

3. *Singular noun:* ____________________

   Plural noun: ____________________

4. *Singular noun:* ____________________

   Plural noun: ____________________

5. *Singular noun:* ____________________

   Plural noun: ____________________

6. *Singular noun:* ____________________

   Plural noun: ____________________

7. *Singular noun:* ____________________

   Plural noun: ____________________

8. *Singular noun:* ____________________

   Plural noun: ____________________

Learning Language **Tell a partner a sentence that uses the singular and plural form of the same noun. Have your partner identify the plural rule you used. (Don't use the words above.)**

ELPS 4C

Abbreviations

An **abbreviation** is a shorter way to write a word or phrase—a shortcut! (See *Write Source* pages 566 and 568.)

Example

Dr. Wilson watches *ER* on his big *TV*.
(*Dr.* is an abbreviation for *Doctor. ER* is an abbreviation for *emergency room. TV* is an abbreviation for *television.*)

Find all the words that can be abbreviated and change them to their shortened form. *Hint:* You'll find 11. The first one has been done for you.

Our neighbor, ~~Mister~~ *Mr.* Wilson, asked me to help him move his television tomorrow. It's lucky I know the way to his house! I won't have to use our global positioning system. I'll take my portable compact disc player along.

Mr. Wilson used to work for the Central Intelligence Agency in Washington, District of Columbia. He's funny! His son works in a hospital, so Mister Wilson calls him Doctor Wilson. But he calls me Doctor Franklin, too, even though I'm only nine. Mister Wilson has given me a great idea, though! I think I'll check over Doctor Doolittle, the Wilsons' cat. Here, kitty, kitty!

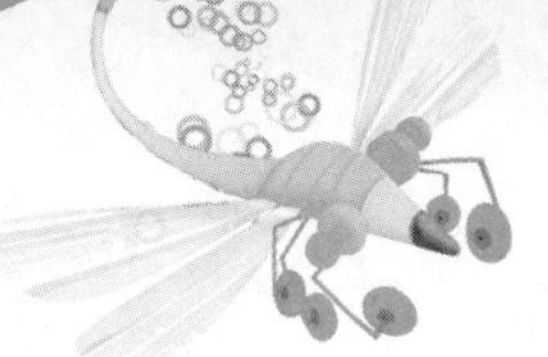

ELPS 4C, 5G

Directions **Match the following terms to their correct abbreviations.**

____	1. C.E.	**a.** kilometer
____	2. PO Box	**b.** for your information
____	3. ATM	**c.** senior
____	4. mpg	**d.** the Common Era
____	5. oz.	**e.** post office box
____	6. p.	**f.** automatic teller machine
____	7. a.m.	**g.** miles per gallon
____	8. Sr.	**h.** ante meridiem (before noon)
____	9. FYI	**i.** ounce
____	10. km	**j.** page

Directions **Fill in each blank with the correct abbreviation from the list.**

Jr. lb. etc. mph M.D. Mrs. p.m. Dr.

Avery Madson, _____, rushed to the hospital. He was clocked at 50 _____, which was too fast, against the law, unwise, _____ The officer who stopped _____ Madson gave him a police escort after he heard it was an emergency. At 11:59 _____, just before midnight, _____ Madson gave birth to an 8-_____ baby boy, Avery Madson, _____ !

The Next Step **On your own paper, write a humorous or exciting story. Use as many abbreviations as you can. Exchange stories with a partner and check to see that you've each used correct abbreviations.**

ELPS 4C

Numbers

When you use **numbers** in your writing, you write them as either numerals or words. Numbers from one to nine are written as words. Larger numbers are written as numbers. Use a combination of numbers and words for very large numbers, like 12 million. Always write out a number that begins a sentence. Dates, times, addresses, pages, and statistics are always written as numerals.

Examples

My class has *26* students in it. *Twenty* of us ride the bus.

In the sentences below, all the numbers are written as words. Some of them should be written as numerals. Using the rules above, find the numbers that should be written as numerals and change them. The first sentence has been done for you.

1. There are three kids in our family, ages ~~nine~~ 9, ~~eleven~~ 11, and ~~thirteen~~ 13.
2. New York City has a population of eight million eight thousand people.
3. Tokyo is even larger with eleven point eight million people.
4. Eight people got on the bus at fourteen twenty Main Street.
5. We were assigned fifteen problems on pages three to five.
6. On April seven, two thousand four, I turned nine years old.
7. Sixteen kids in our class got one hundred percent on the spelling test.
8. The six children had a total of eleven cavities at their checkup.
9. My uncle raised nine children on a forty-acre farm in Minnesota.
10. There are more than two hundred million people in the United States.

ELPS 4C

Directions **Replace words with numerals where needed in the story below.**

In nineteen-o-nine, gold was discovered in Iditarod, Alaska. Iditarod was six hundred twenty-nine trail miles west of what is now Anchorage. In nineteen ten, the United States constructed a winter trail through Iditarod and all the way to Nome, another mining town. During the long winters, sled dogs pulled mail and supplies to the towns along the trail. One sled dog can pull many times its own weight.

To keep this history alive, the Iditarod Trail Sled Dog Race was first held in 1967. It was a short race, covering only twenty-seven miles of the one thousand one hundred fifty-mile trail. The winning musher and dog team won $ twenty-five thousand. After another short race in 1969, the organizers planned a nineteen seventy-three race all the way to Nome. Nowadays, teams leave Anchorage at two-minute intervals, beginning at ten a.m. on the first Saturday in March. Those who finish the race usually reach Nome in 10 to seventeen days. The 1995 winner finished in 9 days, two hours, and forty-two minutes.

Summer hours for the Iditarod Headquarters in Wasilla, Alaska, are mid-May to mid-September, 8:00 a.m. to seven p.m., seven days a week. Tourists can take dog-cart rides between nine a.m. and 6:00 p.m.

ELPS 4C

Spelling Practice

Catching your spelling errors takes practice. Proofreading is the final review you give your writing before sharing your final copy. (See pages 570–575 in *Write Source*.)

In the following story, label the underlined words as "C" for correct, or cross out the word and write the correct spelling above. Also circle the incorrect spellings that a computer spell checker would *not* catch. The first sentence has been done for you.

Just a few (C) blocks from our city ~~naborhood~~ neighborhood, a stand of hardwood trees separates us from the highway. When we ride our bikes too the woods, we inhale the fresh hair as we get closer. A massive, old oak tree stands majestically amung smaller trees, bushs, and wildflowers. Its trunk is so wide around, none of us can put our arms arround it! Its bark forms diffrent patterns as it crawls up the tree, and the tips of its branchs reach for the summar sky. We climb this tree offen, feeling its strength as we sit on its enormus limbs. On a windy day, smaller branchs will sudenly brake off with a crack as the leafs rustle aginst one another.

Spelling Strategies

Here are some ways to help you remember how to spell a word.

Examples

Use Sayings:

PRINCIPAL - I have a pal in the principal.

Make Up an Acrostic (Funny Sentence):

GEOGRAPHY - Giraffes eat old, green rice and paint houses yellow.

Use Familiar Words:

two ➔ twin

sign ➔ signature

Follow the instructions in each of the sentences below.

1. Make up a saying to help you remember how to spell the word "balloon."

____

____

____

2. Create an acrostic for the word "courtesy."

____

____

3. Explain why it is easy to spell "government" when you know how to spell "govern."

____

____

____

ELPS 4C

Spelling with Suffixes 1

If a word ends with a *silent e,* drop the *e* before adding a suffix (ending) that begins with a vowel.

Examples

use ➜ using ➜ usable

nine ➜ ninety

(Don't drop the *e* when the suffix begins with a consonant.)

Add the suffixes as indicated to the following words that end in *silent* e. The first one has been done for you.

	-ing	-ment
1. advertise	*advertising*	*advertisement*
2. encourage		
3. achieve		

	-able	-ing
4. believe		
5. advise		
6. love		

	-ive	-ion
7. decorate		
8. cooperate		
9. operate		

ELPS 4C

Spelling with Suffixes 2

When a one-syllable word with a short vowel needs the ending *-ed, -er,* or *-ing,* the final consonant is usually doubled. (See *Write Source* page 570.)

Example

drop ➜ dropped ➜ dropper ➜ dropping

Directions **Complete the story by filling in each blank with the correct spelling of the word in parentheses.**

My friend Sal and I ____________ *(plan + ed)* to go fishing. She said she could catch a ____________ *(big + er)* fish than I could, and soon we were ____________ *(dig + ing)* in the backyard for worms. We ____________ *(grab + ed)* our tackle and started ____________ *(run + ing)* toward the lake.

"Come on!" Sal yelled. "I've got to catch a ____________ *(whop + er)*!" We both ____________ *(step + ed)* onto the pier and found a place to fish. Sal ____________ *(hum + ed)* as she baited her hook. Worms squirmed on our hooks, turtles were ____________ *(sun + ing)* nearby, and suddenly both ____________ *(bob + er + s)* dunked deep.

"Hah!" Sal said as she was ____________ *(set + ing)* the hook.

"Just wait," I said, and pulled up hard. We each had a fish. Which was ____________ *(big + er)* didn't matter. The fish ____________ *(flip + ed)* and ____________ *(flop + ed)*. When we finally ____________ *(net + ed)* them, we high-fived each other and ____________ *(slip + ed)* the fish back into the lake.

Spelling Rules 1

Some words have letters that you do not pronounce. These are called **silent letters**.

Examples

write	half
foreign	doubt
light	know

Refer to "Improving Spelling" on *Write Source* pages 570–575. Circle the misspelled word in each sentence. Then write the correct spelling of the word on the line. The first one has been done for you.

climbs 1. Joshua's cat always (clims) into open dresser drawers.

______ 2. After Shawn rote her letter, she drew flowers around the border.

______ 3. Dad stores his ice-fishing shed on an iland all summer.

______ 4. Glenna enjoys lisening to crickets chirping at night.

______ 5. Reba knew the anser to the "Question of the Day."

______ 6. The steaming hot coco is buried in marshmallows.

______ 7. Ants scurried away with crums leftover from our picnic.

______ 8. Falling leaves, apple pies, and monarch butterflies remind me of autum.

ELPS 4C

Spelling Rules 2

To make plurals of most words that end in *y*, change *y* to *i* and add *-es*. If the word ends in a vowel plus *y*, just add *-s*.

Examples

bully ➜ bullies   country ➜ countries

toy ➜ toys   monkey ➜ monkeys

To spell words with *i* and *e* together, remember this: "*i* before *e*, except after *c*, or when rhyming with *say*, as in *neighbor* and *weigh*."

Examples

believe   receive   sleigh

Some exceptions: either   weird   heir

(See *Texas Write Source* page 570 for more information on these rules.)

Write "C" for correct if a word is spelled correctly. Otherwise, spell the word correctly.

1. ________________ pullys
2. ________________ boyes
3. ________________ fries
4. ________________ ladys
5. ________________ crys
6. ________________ freight
7. ________________ wieght
8. ________________ joyes
9. ________________ niether
10. ________________ acheive
11. ________________ alleys
12. ________________ wayes
13. ________________ beleif
14. ________________ beautys
15. ________________ citys
16. ________________ communities
17. ________________ bodyes
18. ________________ freind

ELPS 4C

Spelling Review 1

You can avoid many spelling errors by learning a few basic spelling rules. (See page 570 and also review the plurals rules on pages 562 and 564 in *Write Source*.)

Use the list of spelling words beginning on *Write Source* page 572. Add at least three words to each list below.

Words that end in *y* and their plurals

emergency *emergencies*

Words with a doubled consonant before a suffix

getting

Words that have the vowels *i* and *e* together

receive

Words that have dropped a silent *e* before a suffix

judgment

Spelling Review 2

In the following story, label the underlined words as "C" for correct or cross out the word and write the correct spelling above.

This is a wierd story, so I dout that you will beleive it. My mom was beting me that I woud niether dye my hair nor have the curage to let my dad cut it. I decidded not to get into an arguement over it, and just went about my busyness. Then it happined. My brother suddenly droped two pieces of jelly-covered toast on my head. The differnt jellys (grape and raspberry) stuck to my hair, includeing crums from the toast. The gooey, sticky mess driped down my neck!

My dad came along and looked at me. He raised his eyebrows and plopped strait down in his chair. "I wanted to ask you if you needed a haircut, but I see you're geting a dye job first," he laffed.

Since there were no artifisial ingredients in the jellies, at least I could say my hair color was natchral! The jelly did stain my hair for a few days, and I received plenty of admireing comments.

ELPS 2H, 3G, 4C, 5B

Using the Right Word 1

Many words are commonly misused in writing. Learn to use the following words correctly in your writing. (See *Write Source* page 576.)

Examples

Wear **a** raincoat.
Bring **an** umbrella.

We were **allowed** to go outside.
Don't read **aloud** in the library.

Please **accept** this gift.
Everyone **except** Rainy was there.

I saw **a lot** (not **alot**) of pigeons in the park.

For any underlined word that is incorrect, write the correct word above it. Do not change a word that is correct. The first one has been done for you.

a lot

Getting angry can cause alot of trouble. William Kennedy learned a lesson about this during a baseball game. Kennedy was pitching for Brooklyn. He thought he had thrown an strike, but the umpire didn't agree. Kennedy couldn't except the umpire's call. He got mad, yelled, and then threw a ball at the umpire. It missed, accept the umpire said the ball was in play, and the base runners were aloud to head for home plate! An runner scored, and a lot of upset fans watched Brooklyn lose the game. After hearing this story, my brother wondered allowed if that's why people called Kennedy "Roaring Bill."

Learning Language **Write a sentence using each word correctly. Trade papers with a partner and check each other's work. Then tell a partner a new sentence using two words from the top of the page correctly.**

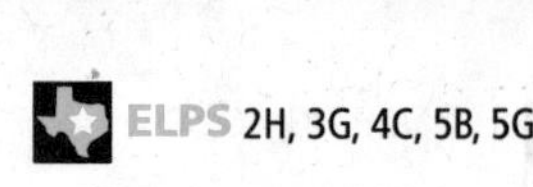

Using the Right Word 2

Check the list of commonly misused words in your *Write Source* book (pages 576–580) to be sure you are using words correctly.

Examples

An **ant** is a tiny insect.
My **aunt** loves me.

We **ate** carrots.
Sarah is **eight** years old.

The **bare** wall needs pictures.
Here's a photo of a grizzly **bear**.

The sky is **blue**.
The wind **blew** hard.

The **brake** will stop the bike.
A short rest period is a **break**.
Be careful not to **break** the window.

We left Scruffy **by** the tree.
Let's **buy** him a chew toy.

You **may** go to the party
if you **can** find a ride.

For each sentence, fill in the blanks below with the correct word from those given in parentheses. (Sometimes, you may have to use a plural word.)

1. My two aunts took ________ friends and me to the zoo for my birthday. We ________ a picnic lunch under a shade tree. *(eight, ate)*
2. We walked ________ a pond to a ________ booth. A breeze ________ as we waited to ________ tickets for the zoo train. *(by, buy; blew, blue)*
3. My ________ pointed to aardvarks eating ________ . *(ants, aunts)*
4. We saw a huge polar ________, covered with thick, white fur except for its nose and the soles of its feet, which were ________. *(bear, bare)*
5. Later, Stacy asked, "________ we get off the train and walk around?" Aunt Marie said, "I'm not sure we ________." *(may, can)*

Learning Language **Write a few sentences about a trip. Use these words correctly: *ant, eight, bare, brake.* Then tell a partner two sentences using two more words from the top of the page.**

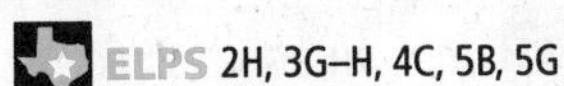
ELPS 2H, 3G–H, 4C, 5B, 5G

Using the Right Word 3

Some words are misused in writing. (See *Write Source* pages 580 and 582.)

Examples

One **cent** is a penny.
Perfume has a sweet **scent**.
Mom **sent** me a valentine.

Sean **chose** Mark for the team.
He will **choose** Tina next.

Just **close** the door.
My **clothes** are dirty.

A **creak** is a squeaky sound.
Don't drink the water in the **creek**.

Oh **dear**, stop the car!
The **deer** grazed near the road.

Scorpions live in the **desert**.
The **dessert** was gooey.

Cindy wants to **dye** her hair.
We didn't want our sick cat to **die**.

Directions

For any underlined word that is incorrect, write the correct word above it. Do not change a word that is correct. The first one has been done for you.

dessert

"What should we have for desert?" asked Mabel. "Yesterday we choose fruit, but today let's choose frozen yogurt!" Soon I was scent to get some frozen yogurt. The cent of raspberries always fills the store, and the old floorboards creak.

"Hi, deer! What'll it be?" asked the clerk. Her close were clean under her smudged apron. "I should die this apron red to match the berry spills," she laughed. I ordered raspberry swirl. For a dollar and a few scents, she gave me a single-dip cone. I remembered to clothes the door behind me.

Learning Language **Write a story about a picnic. Use these words correctly: *deer, creek, sent, dessert, clothes*. Tell a partner a story using two more words from the top of the page.**

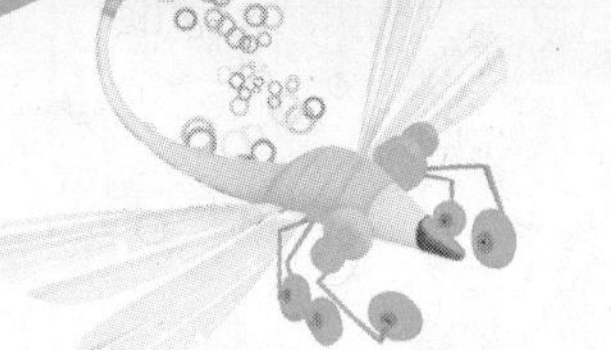

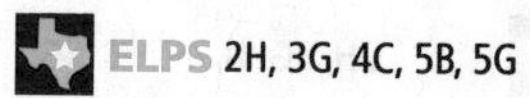

Using the Right Word 4

Many words are easily confused in writing. Learn to use the following words correctly. (See *Write Source* pages 582 and 584.)

Examples

They **don't** like liver.
He **doesn't** like it either.

Four plus **four** is eight.
Wait here **for** a while.

Mmm, this is **good** cake.
You bake very **well**.

A **hare** looks like a rabbit.
My **hair** needs cutting.

There is a **hole** in this sock.
Will you watch the **whole** game?

Come **here**, please.
Did you **hear** me?

For any underlined word that is incorrect, write the correct word above. Do not change correct words. The first one has been done for you.

An adult male African elephant weighs over 12,000 pounds, more than for *four* compact cars! Even a hippopotamus don't outweigh the elephant. (A male hippo in good health only weighs about 8,000 pounds.) Because an elephant is a mammal, it has hare or fur. Its tail serves the elephant good as a fly swatter. Have you ever heard an elephant's trumpeting roar? Elephants can also make sounds so low that people don't here them. And hear is another amazing fact: Elephants many miles away actually here these deep tones. African elephants live in groups called herds. Their large ears doesn't flap for nothing, either. They are used four cooling their whole bodies.

Learning Language **Write about an animal, using these words correctly: *don't, for, doesn't, well, hair, here.* Tell a partner a sentence using *hole* or *whole* and one other word from the list.**

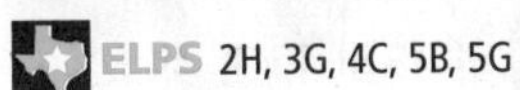
ELPS 2H, 3G, 4C, 5B, 5G

Using the Right Word 5

Some words are misused in writing. (See *Write Source* page 584.)

Examples

I broke the **heel** of my shoe.
It takes time for cuts to **heal**.

The show lasts an **hour**.
Come over to **our** house.

The cat licked **its** fur.
I know **it's** time to eat.

I want to **learn** to knit.
My friend Ana will **teach** me.

My brother's tooth is **loose**.
Don't **lose** my lucky penny.

Did you **meet** my sister?
Ham is my favorite **meat**.

For any underlined word that is incorrect, write the correct word above it. Do not change a word that is correct.

The whole world knows that lightning is dangerous. When the sky flashes and booms, hour first thought should be to take cover. Lightning storms travel at about 25 miles per hour, so you should not stay outside to watch the storm. Learn people to get in the house! Its the safest place to be. Try to stay away from lose objects that might fall on you. Bruises take a while to heel. Be prepared to lose power. The *Guinness Book of Records* tells about people who have survived lightning strikes. It's facts will amaze you! I'd like to meat someone who's been hit by lightning. That would be an interesting story.

Learning Language **Write a story about a storm you remember or heard about. Use the following words correctly in your writing: *lose, hour, heel, its, teach, learn*. Then tell a partner a sentence using two more words from the list at the top of the page.**

ELPS 2H, 3G, 4C, 5B

Using the Right Word 6

Some words sound alike or are easily confused for some other reason. Refer to *Write Source* page 586 for more information.

Examples

Magnets stick to **metal**.
I won a **medal** at the race.

A coal **miner** digs for coal.
That **minor** dent is easy to fix.

She has **one** brother.
He **won** a trophy.

A raindrop hit the window **pane**.
My broken toe caused me **pain**.

We walked **past** Lila's house.
The player **passed** the ball.

Leave Mom in **peace** and quiet.
This puzzle **piece** belongs here.

For any underlined word that is incorrect, write the correct word above it. Do not change a word that is correct.

The modern Olympics were started as a way to promote piece around the world. Athletes from all over the world compete for metals in the Olympic Games. Prizes are made of different metals: gold, bronze, and silver. Miners must hope that the gold they find becomes a piece of Olympic history. I wonder which country has won the most? I saw a relay race in track and field. The runner tripped and dropped the baton as he past it to the next runner. What seemed like one miner error cost his team the race when another runner passed him. The memory of that mistake must cause him pane.

Learning Language **Write sentences using the following words correctly: *metal, one, pain, past, piece*. Then tell a partner several sentences using three more words from the list at the top of the page.**

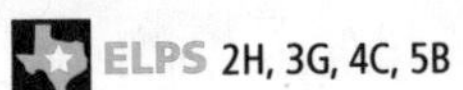
ELPS 2H, 3G, 4C, 5B

Using the Right Word 7

Some words sound alike or are confused for some other reason. Refer to *Write Source* page 588 for more information.

Examples

The school principal is Ms. Smith.
In principle, I play to have fun.

I am quite sleepy.
Please be quiet.
Let's quit raking.

The students raise their hands.
Rays from the sun kept me warm.

Mom read the paper today.
Red is Maria's favorite color.

What is the actress's real name?
We were really tired.

What was the right answer?
She can write very neatly.

Underline the correct choice in each set of parentheses.

1. The Olympic Games are *(quit / quiet / quite)* important to amateur athletes, so they work hard and don't *(quit / quiet / quite)*.
2. In *(principle / principal)*, countries all get along during the games.
3. Winners watch as officials *(raise / rays)* the flag of their country.
4. I *(read / red)* that the torch relay was not always part of the Olympics.
5. Since 1936, the torch relay has been a *(real / really)* popular addition.
6. I think adding the torch relay was the *(right / write)* decision.
7. I like the countries with *(read / red)* uniforms the best.
8. Athletes must show *(real / really)* commitment to make the Olympics.

Learning Language **Write sentences using these words: *right, rays, red, quiet.* Then tell a partner a short story using three more words from the list at the top of the page.**

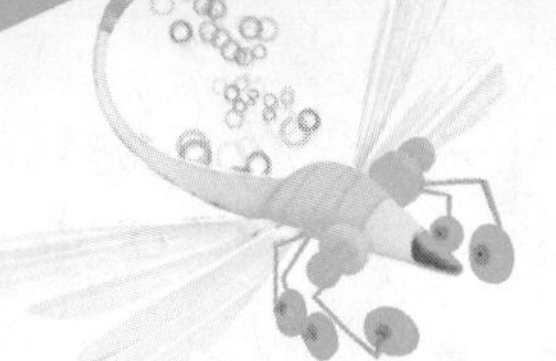

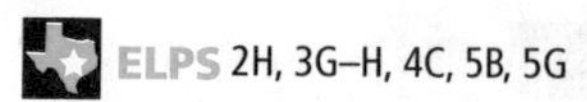

ELPS 2H, 3G–H, 4C, 5B, 5G

Using the Right Word 8

Always check your writing to be sure you have used the right words. See *Write Source* page 590 for a list of commonly misused words.

Examples

Which movie **scene** was best?
Have you **seen** my sweater?

The **sea** is wavy today.
Do you **see** the ship?

The dogs **seem** nervous.
Your sleeve **seam** is ripped.

A tailor can **sew** clothes.
Turn on the light **so** I can see.
I will **sow** sunflower seeds today.

Let's **sit** on the porch.
Please **set** the chair there.

Nan baked **some** cookies.
The **sum** of 2+2 is 4.

Dad's **son** is my brother.
The **sun** will rise at 5:05 a.m.

Directions **Underline the correct word from those in parentheses.**

1. While the ladies *(sit / set)* and *(so / sew / sow)* the *(seems / seams)* of the quilt squares, they tell stories.
2. It would *(seam / seem)* that many people are afraid of bats.
3. If you've *(seen / scene)* movies where bats look mean, it's not true.
4. Bats are good; *(sum / some)* can eat 1,000 mosquitoes in an hour!
5. After the *(son / sun)* goes down, many bats come out to feed.
6. They *(see / sea)* in the dark by using built-in sonar called "echolocation."
7. Watching bats in flight is quiet a *(seen / scene)*.

Learning Language **Write a paragraph about an interesting animal. Use the following words correctly in your writing: *scene, see, so, set, some, sun*. Then tell a partner about an animal using two more words from the top of the page.**

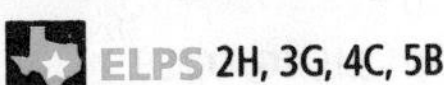
ELPS 2H, 3G, 4C, 5B

Using the Right Word 9

Study these commonly misused words. (See *Write Source* page 592 for more information.)

Examples

Did Scruffy steal my cookie?
Steel is a very strong metal.

Scruffy wags his tail.
Grandpa told us a tall tale.

Look over there.
They're making a movie.
Don't bump their cameras.

I'd rather swim than run.
Then we'll play tag.

We paged through the album.
Juan threw a fast curveball.

The wind is too cold.
Come inside to read.
We have two new books.

Directions **Underline the correct choice within each set of parentheses.**

1. For Venus flytraps, *(there / their)* diet as houseplants consists of *(too / two / to)* houseflies per month.

2. If you give Venus flytraps a bit of meat rather *(then / than)* an insect, the plants may start *(two / too / to)* die.

3. In the flytrap, *(they're / there)* are sensitive hairs on the leaves. When an insect bends the hairs, the leaf snaps shut like a *(steal / steel)* trap.

4. *(Threw / Through)* the years, science-fiction writers have told some scary *(tails / tales)* about giant, man-eating plants.

5. Of course, these stories aren't true, but a large tropical pitcher plant may be able *(too / two / to)* trap a frog or *(too / two / to)*.

6. In the pitcher plant, an insect falls into a vase-like leaf, and *(than / then)* it cannot crawl out because the walls are *(two / too / to)* slippery.

Learning Language **Write three sentences using these words correctly: *there, tail, threw.* Tell a partner a sentence using two more words from the list at the top of the page.**

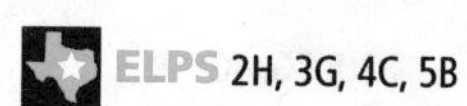

ELPS 2H, 3G, 4C, 5B

Using the Right Word 10

Review these misused words on *Write Source* pages 592 and 594.

Examples

Hey, **wait** for me!
Check the dog's **weight**.

Don't **waste** water.
These pants are tight in the **waist**.

Do you know the **way**?
What did Scruffy **weigh**?

Dad is **weak** after being sick for a **week**.

In the story, the **witch** is banished.
Which book did you like best?

We need **wood** for a campfire.
Jack said he **would** cut some.

You're right on time!
Let me take **your** coat.

Directions **Cross out only the incorrect words and write the correct words above.**

1. Witch would way more on a spaceship to Mars . . . you're science teacher or your pet mouse? (Think about it.)
2. This weak's tongue twister: How much would wood a woodchuck chuck?
3. Do you know the rules, "Clean you're plate" and "Waist not, want not"?
4. Overdoing these rules could lead to waste and wait problems.
5. My brother felt week. After lifting waits for a weak, he had gained weight.
6. Muscles way more than fat, so someone who lifts waits wood be heavier than a person of the same size who just sits around.
7. Check you're answer to the first question. They would both weigh zero.

Learning Language **Write three sentences using these words correctly: *waste, which, wood, your.* Tell a partner a sentence using two more of the words from the list at the top of the page.**

ELPS 4C, 5B

Using the Right Word Review

Directions **Choose the correct word from each pair to fill in the blanks below.**

1. Because you were sick, *(your / you're)* ______________ going to have to make up *(your / you're)* ______________ homework.

2. We walked *(threw / through)* ______________ the mall, but we didn't *(by / buy)* ___________ anything.

3. My hat is so *(lose / loose)* ______________ , I'll probably *(lose / loose)* ______________ it in this wind!

4. My parents parked *(there / their)* ____________ car *(by / buy)* ________ the gym.

5. Our class is going on *(its / it's)* _________ spring field trip tomorrow.

6. The flu left Dad too *(weak / week)* ______________ to go to work for a whole *(weak / week)* ______________ .

7. Terry *(threw / through)* ______________ the baseball into those bushes over *(there / their)* ______________ .

8. In an *(our / hour)* __________, *(our / hour)* __________ bus should arrive.

9. The soccer team *(one / won)* _________ *(its / it's)* _________ first game today.

10. *(Its / It's)* ________ getting *(to / too)* ________ dark *(to / too)* ________ see.

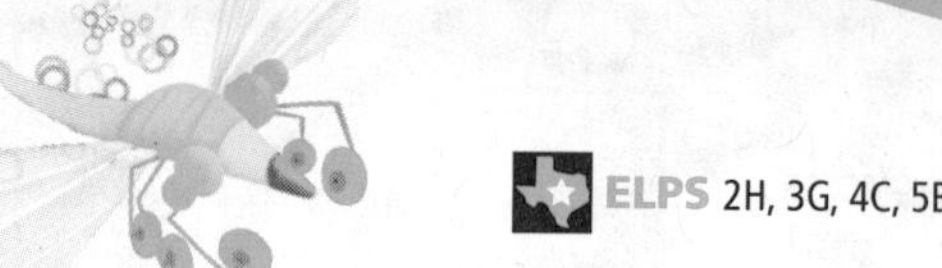

ELPS 2H, 3G, 4C, 5B

Directions Fill in each blank with the correct word.

1. Ms. Lee told a tall ___________ about a cat with a 20-foot ___________. *(tail / tale)*

2. There was no ___________ my dog would let us ___________ him. *(way / weigh)*

3. The wind ___________ the clouds away, leaving a clear ___________ sky. *(blue / blew)*

4. The ___________ of us easily ___________ the large pizza. *(ate / eight)*

5. Diego's sore ___________ will ___________ quickly. *(heel / heal)*

6. In the ___________, we've ___________ the bakery without stopping. *(past / passed)*

7. My ___________ bought me an ___________ farm. *(ant / aunt)*

8. She won't ___________ down from the ___________. *(peak / peek)*

Learning Language On your own paper, use the word pairs below correctly in the same sentence. One has been done for you.

allowed/aloud one/won here/hear for/four

We're not **allowed** to talk **aloud** in the library.

Then tell a partner two sentences using these word pairs correctly:

steal/steel witch/which

Sentence Activities

The activities in this section cover four important areas: (1) the basic parts, types, and kinds of sentences, (2) the methods for writing smooth-reading sentences; (3) common sentence errors; and (4) ways to add variety to sentences. Most activities contain a main practice part, in which you review, combine, or analyze sentences. In addition, The Next Step and Learning Language activities give you follow-up practice with certain skills.

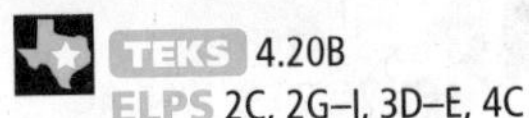
TEKS 4.20B
ELPS 2C, 2G–I, 3D–E, 4C

Simple and Complete Subjects

The **simple subject** is the part of a sentence that is doing something. The **complete subject** is the simple subject and all the words that describe it. (See *Write Source* page 596.) *Hint:* Sometimes the simple subject stands alone.

Examples

Simple Subject: Marc skis often.

Complete Subject: Marc, who loves snow, skis often.

In each sentence below, circle the simple subject. Then underline the complete subject.

1. Catherine visited a castle not far from Paris.
2. Roy, Catherine's friend, built a rocket out of cat-food cans.
3. Rocky, a raccoon, rode Roy's rocket to the moon.
4. A moon monster wearing a cowboy hat roared at Rocky.
5. The hungry monster ate Rocky's rocket.
6. Randy, the flying squirrel, flew Rocky back home.
7. Catherine invited Randy and Rocky to the castle for crêpes.

Learning Language **On your own paper, write three funny sentences of your own. In each sentence, circle the simple subject and underline the complete subject. Exchange papers with a classmate and check each other's work. Then tell a partner a new sentence and have your partner identify the simple subject and the complete subject.**

Simple and Complete Predicates

The **simple predicate** (verb) is the part of a sentence that tells what the subject is doing. The **complete predicate** is the simple predicate and all the words that describe it. (See *Write Source* page 598.)

Example

Simple Predicate: My house has a big backyard.

Complete Predicate: My house has a big backyard.

In each sentence below, circle the simple predicate. Then underline the complete predicate. The first one has been done for you.

1. Doug (is) my little brother.
2. He is digging a hole in the backyard.
3. He plans to dig all the way to China.
4. He works on the hole every day.
5. Mom saw the hole last Friday.
6. She asked Doug a lot of questions.
7. He got our dad to help him on Saturday.
8. Mom laughed for a long time after that!

Learning Language **On your own paper, write three sentences about your own brother or sister, or about a friend. Circle the simple predicate and underline the complete predicate in each sentence. Then tell a partner a new sentence. Have your partner identify the complete predicate.**

ELPS 4C, 5F

Compound Subjects and Predicates

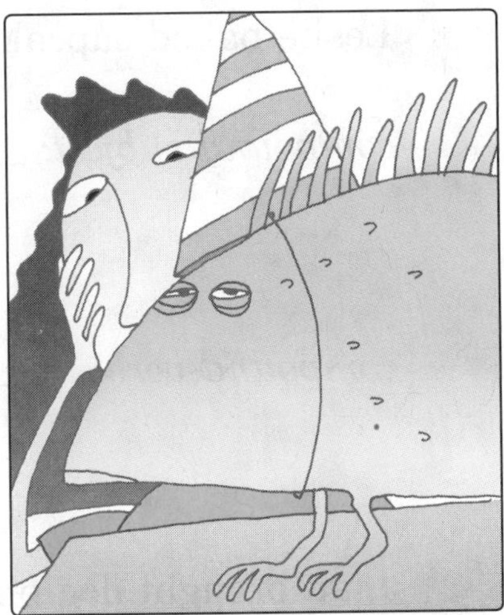

You already know that every sentence needs a subject and a verb. However, a sentence may have more than one subject and more than one verb. **Compound subjects** and **compound predicates** (verbs) are explained on *Write Source* pages 596 and 598.

Example

Jake and Mitch raise and sell guppies.

Rewrite each of the following sentences two times. First change the sentence so that it has a compound subject. Then change the sentence so that it has a compound verb. Underline your subjects once and your verbs twice. The first one has been done for you.

1. Our class had a pet party.

   compound subject: Our class and Mrs. Nathan's class had a pet party.

   compound verb: Our class had a pet party and learned about animals.

2. Stacy held the gerbils.

   compound subject: ______________________

   compound verb: ______________________

ELPS 4C, 5F

3. Leslie baked cupcakes.

compound subject: ______________________________

____

compound verb: ______________________________

____

4. Juan brought dog biscuits and carrots.

compound subject: ______________________________

____

compound verb: ______________________________

____

The Next Step **Write one sentence using a compound subject and one sentence using a compound verb. Exchange your sentences with a classmate and check each other's work.**

compound subject:

____

____

compound verb:

____

____

ELPS 4C

Clauses

A **clause** is a group of related words that has both a subject and a predicate. An **independent clause** expresses a complete thought and can stand alone as a sentence. A **dependent clause** does not express a complete thought and cannot stand alone. (See *Write Source* page 600.)

Examples

Independent Clause: Scott kicked a goal.

Dependent Clause: After Scott kicked a goal

Directions **On the line before each clause, write "D" if it is a dependent clause and "I" if it is an independent clause. Add the correct end punctuation for each independent clause. The first one has been done for you.**

___I___ 1. Something is wrong with our computer.

______ 2. Our class is going to a concert

______ 3. While you are at the library

______ 4. Because I have a spelling test tomorrow

______ 5. That Jerry wrote

______ 6. I called Josie

______ 7. Since Ray was late

______ 8. Until I finish my homework

______ 9. Let's go

______ 10. Can you reach that shelf

______ 11. That Sharon bought

ELPS 4C, 5F

Each sentence below has one independent clause and one dependent clause. Underline the independent clause, and circle the dependent clause. The first one has been done for you.

1. Before the movie started, I got some popcorn.
2. I got a good grade because I studied last night.
3. We stayed inside until the storm passed.
4. Whatever we do, let's get something to eat soon.
5. Yesterday my next-door neighbor gave me five old records that he bought when he was a teenager.
6. He also gave me a phonograph, which I need to play them.
7. If the snow doesn't stop soon, we won't have school tomorrow.
8. I ride my bike to school unless it is raining.

The Next Step **Complete the following sentences by adding an independent clause to each dependent clause.**

1. While my parents talked to my teacher, ______________________________

____

2. Because it was dark, ______________________________

____

3. When the bell rang, ______________________________

____

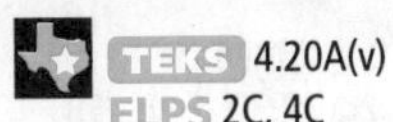
TEKS 4.20A(v)
ELPS 2C, 4C

Prepositional Phrases 2

You know that **prepositional phrases** can provide details in sentences. Some of those details tell about location, time, or direction. (See *Write Source* pages 60? and 632.)

Examples

A cat is on top of the desk.
(This prepositional phrase includes the compound preposition *on top of*, the noun object *desk*, and the adjective *the*.)

Another cat lies under it.

On warm days, she sleeps there.

One cat has crawled into a drawer.

Each sentence below contains a prepositional phrase. Underline it and then write whether it shows location, time, or direction. The first sentence has been done for you.

1. Ginger and Jazz are sleeping on my bed. *location*
2. In a few minutes I will fix their breakfast. ________
3. The can opener's sound makes them run toward the kitchen. ________
4. Sometimes Ginger stands silently next to me. ________
5. Usually, though, she sits by the door and meows impatiently. ________
6. She would go into our refrigerator if she could! ________
7. Jazz watches me but acts bored during Ginger's performance. ________

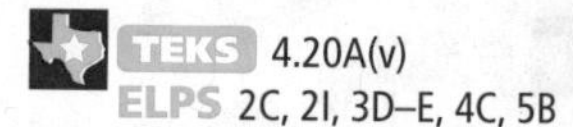

The Next Step **Now write sentences using at least four prepositional phrases that show time, location, or direction. Underline the prepositional phrases you used. One has been done for you.**

1. *I put my books <u>on my bed</u> and patted Ginger.*

2. ______________________________

3. ______________________________

4. ______________________________

5. ______________________________

Learning Language **Ask a partner to answer these questions. Each response should use a prepositional phrase. Where do the cats play? When are they most active? Where do they like to go for a nap? Talk about the answers. Decide which prepositional phrases tell about location, time, or direction.**

ELPS 4C

Sentence Fragments 2

In this activity, you will practice correcting **sentence fragments.** (See *Write Source* page 474.)

Example

Fragment:
Live in the Arctic.
(A subject is missing.)

Sentence:
The Inuit people live in the Arctic.
(A subject is added.)

On each line below, put an "S" if the words that follow make a sentence. Put an "F" if they make a sentence fragment. The first one has been marked for you. (There are seven fragments.)

___F___ 1. Called the Inuit "Eskimos."

_______ 2. The word "Inuit" means "the people."

_______ 3. Some Inuit used to live in igloos in the winter.

_______ 4. Igloos were made out of blocks of ice and snow.

_______ 5. Clear ice blocks for windows.

_______ 6. Others huts out of whale bones.

_______ 7. Also made one-person boats called "kayaks."

_______ 8. Larger boats called "umiaks."

_______ 9. Made sleds that were pulled by dogs.

_______ 10. The Inuit people have a proud tradition.

_______ 11. Now live in pre-built houses.

ELPS 4C

In the following paragraph, add the words from the list below to turn the fragments into complete sentences. Correct capitalization if necessary.

story	was	English	lived
changed	disagree	Eskimos	

For a long time, many people thought that Eskimos used hundreds of words for "snow." Eskimos with a lot of snow, so the story had to be true. New studies with that idea. Most people who study languages now think that Eskimos have only 18 words for "snow." Has about the same number. How did the get started? Some think that as the story was told and retold, it. Things were added or left out. Lived too far away. It impossible to easily check the truth of the story.

The Next Step **For the fragments on page 95, add words to make them into complete sentences. The first one has been done for you. Complete your work on your own paper.**

1. Explorers called the Inuit "Eskimos."

____

____

ELPS 4C

Run-On Sentences 1

A **run-on sentence** happens when two sentences are joined without punctuation or a connecting word. (See *Write Source* page 475.)

Example

Run-On Sentence:
A fish never shuts its eyes it can't even blink.

Corrected Sentence:
A fish never shuts its eyes. It can't even blink.
(End punctuation and a capital letter make two sentences.)

Correct the run-on sentences below by dividing them into two sentences. Use correct capitalization and end punctuation in your new sentences. The first one has been done for you.

1. Earthworms have 10 hearts. Snails have eyes on stalks.
2. Grasshoppers can jump 30 inches that's like you jumping across a football field.
3. Ants can lift 50 times their weight how much can you lift?
4. Squirrels bury more nuts than they dig up the nuts left in the ground sometimes grow into trees.
5. Birds' wings have feathers bats' wings are skin.
6. Camels drink as much as 30 gallons of water at one time no wonder they can cross deserts.
7. Kangaroo rats rarely drink water they get the water they need from the plants they eat.

ELPS 4C

Directions: Read the following paragraph and correct the run-on sentences. Be sure to use correct capitalization and punctuation where needed.

Crayfish live in streams and lakes lobsters live in the ocean. Lobsters and crayfish belong to the same family of animals they are not related to fish. Lobsters look like giant crayfish. Crayfish have four pairs of legs and a set of pincers. If a pincer is broken off, the crayfish will grow a new one the new pincer will be a lot smaller than the old one. A crayfish has no bones the hard outer shell of the body acts like a skeleton. The crayfish's tail flips quickly to move the animal backward people are often surprised because they expect the animal to move forward.

The Next Step **Write a run-on sentence about animals. Exchange papers with a partner. Correct your partner's run-on sentence by dividing it into separate sentences.**

Run-On Sentence

____

____

____

Corrected Sentence

____

____

____

ELPS 4C

Run-On Sentences 2

In this activity, you'll practice correcting **run-on sentences** by adding a comma and a coordinating conjunction. Here are some conjunctions to choose from: *and, but, so,* and *yet.* (See *Write Source* page 475.)

Example

Run-On Sentence:
Panda bears live in China they eat bamboo.

Corrected Sentence:
Panda bears live in China, and they eat bamboo.

Directions

Correct the run-on sentences below by adding a comma and a conjunction. The first one has been done for you.

1. There are eight basic kinds of bears, and the big brown bears are some of the largest bears in the world.

2. Sun bears are the smallest kind of bear they still weigh 60 to 100 pounds.

3. Polar bears, a third kind, live in the Arctic they are able to swim in very cold water.

4. Their thick fur keeps them warm their front paws work as paddles.

5. Grizzly bears, a fourth kind of bear, used to roam freely in the West now most of them live in national parks.

6. There are American black bears, Asiatic black bears, and spectacled bears don't forget the slow-moving sloth bears.

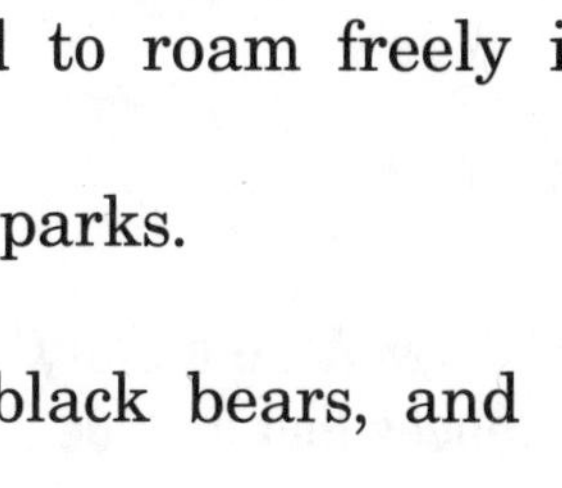

7. A bear travels over a large area during the summer in the winter it stays in a warm den.

8. Bears can outrun people only black bears regularly climb trees.

9. Some scientists say that the brown bear is the largest bear in the world others say that the polar bear is the largest.

10. Most bears eat just about anything they can survive in many different places.

11. Koala bears of Australia are not bears at all they are related to kangaroos.

12. Polar bears' main food is seal the bears have to hunt.

13. Panda bears eat bamboo they don't have to hunt in the same way.

14. Pandas can adapt to some changes the presence of people can also cause starvation.

15. Bears are intelligent they can learn to get food from a campsite.

16. You should avoid feeding bears they can become used to handouts.

17. Bears that eat handouts become dangerous they may have to be killed.

The Next Step **Write a story about bears or another animal of your choice. Try to use at least two sentences that include a comma and a conjunction such as *and, but, so, or,* and *yet*.**

ELPS 4C

Rambling Sentences

A **rambling sentence** happens when several sentences are connected with *and.*

Example

Rambling Sentence:
I got up in a hurry and I ate my cereal and then I got on the school bus and I saw my best friend.

Corrected Sentences:
I got up in a hurry and ate my cereal. Then I got on the school bus and saw my best friend.

Read the rambling sentences that follow. Correct them by dividing them into as many sentences as you think are needed. Cross out the extra *and*'s, capitalize the first letter of each sentence, and use correct end punctuation. The first line has been done for you.

1. Misha and I went to the zoo yesterday. ~~and~~ We saw polar bears, zebras, and elephants and we also saw seals and otters and then we got some juice and rested for a few minutes and finally, we saw the baby animals in the children's zoo and the little llamas were the friendliest babies.

2. My mom went to Japan on a business trip and she called me as soon as she got there and she said it was already Wednesday there even though it was only Tuesday here and I asked her how she could be in a different day and still be talking to me and she said I should ask my science teacher.

ELPS 4C

3. The edges of the Pacific Ocean have many volcanoes and earthquakes and when some of those volcanoes erupt, they can cause many problems for people who live near them and the people have to watch out for lava and ash and they have to use special construction materials to keep buildings from collapsing during an earthquake and they also have to watch for tsunamis, giant waves, that often crash onto the shore after an earthquake happens or a volcano erupts.

4. A long time ago, the Algonquin people built birch bark canoes with frames made of cedar and they sewed the birch bark around the frame with spruce roots and then they sealed the canoe with pine pitch and they used a crooked knife, an axe, and an awl to do all this work and they made canoes that were about eight feet long and they also made canoes that were as long as thirty-seven feet.

The Next Step **On your own paper, write a short story about an unusual lunch. Use *and*'s instead of end punctuation so that you have one long rambling sentence. Then exchange papers with a classmate and correct each other's rambling sentence.**

ELPS 4C

Double Negatives

Double negatives are another kind of sentence problem. Do not use two negatives like *no, not, never,* or *none* in the same sentence.

Example

Double Negative:
My brother hasn't got no pencils.

Corrected Sentence:
My brother hasn't got any pencils.

In the following sentences, change the double negatives so that each sentence is correct. The first one has been done for you.

1. The first pencils weren't ~~no~~ pencils at all.
2. The Romans never used no wood for their writing tools because they used a lead rod.
3. Lead never needed no wood, but soft graphite needed a wooden holder.
4. Most pencils have erasers, but some people don't never use an eraser.
5. If your pencil lead breaks, you can't write nothing until you sharpen it.
6. Colored pencils aren't never meant for writing, but they are great for revising and editing.
7. The teacher hasn't given us no homework today.
8. The teacher said nobody should use no pen for drawing.

The Next Step **Use *not, no, never,* and *nothing* in a four different sentences. Do not use any double negatives.**

ELPS 4C

Sentence Problems Review 1

In this review, you will practice correcting sentence errors you learned about earlier.

Read the following sentences and make corrections where needed. If a sentence is correct, do not change it.

1. Plastic is used for sports helmets motorcycle helmets are plastic, too.
2. Plastic is strong, and it is light and plastic can protect a football player's head.
3. Don't never use a broken or damaged helmet.
4. A plastic batting helmet has a special face guard.
5. Students who play hockey at school must wear protective helmets.
6. Schools don't buy no cheap helmets for their football teams.
7. Many skiers, bicyclists, and skateboarders now wear helmets, too.
8. Some helmets have bright colors other helmets have fancy designs.
9. The plastic in a helmet is very strong and resists breaking.
10. Helmets have vents to let heat escape and they have straps to hold the helmet in place and padding helps protect a person's head and makes the helmet fit better and many people have avoided serious injury thanks to wearing safety helmets.
11. Football rules don't allow no one to play with an unstrapped helmet.

 ELPS 4C

Sentence Problems Review 2

In this activity, you will practice correcting many of the sentence errors you have learned about.

The following paragraph contains sentence fragments, run-on sentences, and other problems. Make each sentence complete and correct. The first correction has been done for you.

But if you do, you are

You may think that dragons live only in fairy tales. Wrong. Really do exist. Komodo dragons aren't no little lizards they are huge. They can grow to be 10 feet long and weigh as much as 300 pounds. Like other reptiles, lay eg[illegible]hough they are big and heavy, Komodo dragons can run very fast [illegible]e lizards can catch small deer, wild pigs, and other small anima[illegible] their bite is deadly. Don't never have to worry about being bi[illegible] by a Komodo dragon unless you live in Indonesia that's where the dragons live. If you would like to see one up close and in person, just go to Komodo Island National Park about 1,000 dragons there.

ELPS 4C

The paragraph below contains run-on and rambling sentences. Correct them by breaking them into shorter sentences. The first one has been done for you.

There are many types of lizards besides Komodo dragons some of them live in the United States and one type of lizard that lives in this country is the Gila monster it is poisonous, and it grows as long as two feet. Gila monsters are slow-moving lizards that live in the desert Southwest and they eat eggs, birds, and rodents and they store fat in their tails so they can live for months without food if they have to. The bite of a Gila monster hurts, but it would not kill a person. Of course there are many kinds of lizards that are harmless and some people even keep lizards as pets and my friend Emily puts her iguana on a leash and takes it everywhere with her. Unlike most other lizards, iguanas eat plants, fruit, and flowers.

TEKS 4.20C
ELPS 2C, 3D, 4C, 5D

Subject-Verb Agreement 1

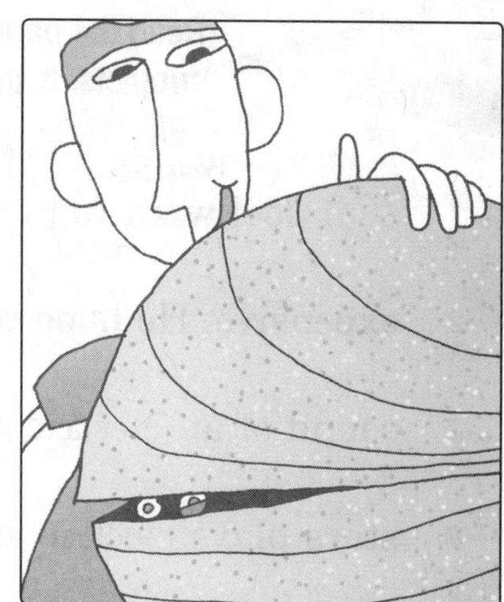

Subject-verb agreement basically means that if the subject of a sentence is singular, the verb must be singular, too. If the subject is plural, the verb must be plural, too. (See *Write Source* page 476.)

Examples

Singular Subject and Verb:
Sheila has a chinchilla.

Plural Subject and Verb:
The students in our class have strange pets.

In the sentences below, cross out the incorrect verb and write the correct one on the line provided. The verb you choose should agree with the subject. The first sentence has been done for you.

1. Two students in our class ~~has~~ iguanas. ___*have*___
2. Jamila have a ferret. __________
3. Ferrets is a lot like weasels. __________
4. Jamila's ferret are named Gizmo. __________
5. He run really fast. __________
6. Jamila's golden retriever Sam love Gizmo. __________
7. They takes naps together. __________
8. Gizmo sneak up on Sam sometimes. __________
9. Then he bite Sam's ears. __________
10. He are just playing, though. __________

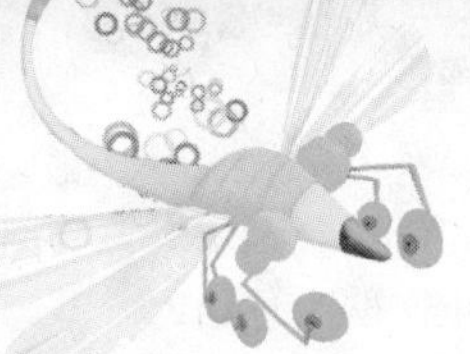

Read the paragraph below and correct the verbs so that they agree with their subjects. If they are already correct, do not change them.

Joel want to buy a guitar. He knows that guitars are very expensive. He hope to find a good used one. Although he like the sound of an electric guitar, he would have to buy an amp. Many rock stars plays electric guitars. Joel's best friend, who has been taking lessons for about two years, say Joel should buy an acoustic guitar. Even if there are no electricity, he can still play and create great music. If he wants, Joel can buy an electric pickup for his acoustic guitar. Salespeople tells Joel that some top performers have acoustic guitars. A music store only six blocks from his house have three good used guitars. Joel have asked his father to help him pick out the right guitar. His father plays guitar and is excited that Joel want to learn how to play. Joel have saved half the cost of the guitar that he wants to buy. If his father agree to pay the rest of the cost, Joel will repay his parents.

Learning Language **Write five sentences about an unusual or imaginary pet. Make sure the subjects and verbs of your sentences agree. Trade papers with a classmate and check each other's work. Then tell a partner a new sentence that uses correct sentence-verb agreement.**

TEKS 4.20C
ELPS 2C, 4C, 5D

Subject-Verb Agreement 2

Subjects and verbs must "agree" in sentences that have compound subjects. (See *Write Source* page 477.) Here are two basic rules you need to know:

1. A compound subject connected by **and** needs a plural verb.
2. A compound subject connected by **or** may need a plural or a singular verb. The verb must agree with the subject that is closer to it.

Using the rules above, correct the following sentences by making the subject and verb agree. At the end of each sentence, write which rule you used. The first two have been done for you.

1. Either the cats or the dog ~~have~~ *has* to go out. *(Rule 2.)*
   The verb agrees with dog, the closer subject.
2. Michelle and Cindy ~~is~~ *are* going to start a band. *(Rule 1.)*
3. Either Tom or Marsha play shortstop.
4. Dan and Amy takes guitar lessons.
5. Chachi and Cindy is the best singers in our school.
6. Cindy's brothers or sister usually sing with her.
7. Charlie's brother or sisters is always yelling at him.
8. Jeff and Darla goes to California every summer.
9. Sue's brothers and cousin plays tennis.
10. Sue's brothers or cousin are coming to pick her up.

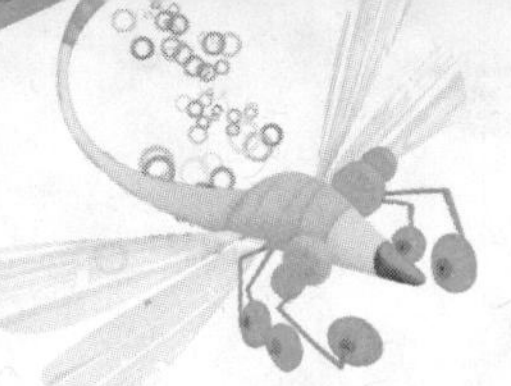

Carefully read the following paragraphs. Do the verbs agree with the subjects? If not, change the verbs using rule 1 or rule 2. If the verbs agree, do not change them.

José loves to paint. However, walls or fences isn't what he paints. Instead, José paints people and animals on canvas. He is taking a class to learn how to paint better. He and the rest of the art students is learning how to mix paint. Paper or canvas are used by most artists. José's cats and dog is part of his first painting assignment. José and one other student decides to share paint supplies during the course.

After a couple weeks of painting in the class, José discovers that oil paints is his favorites. The teacher says that José and the other students is doing very well. She announce an art exhibit as the final project for the class. The students hang their paintings on the library walls.

Learning Language **Using the rules on the previous page, write two sentences that fit rule number 1 and two that fit rule number 2. Exchange papers with a classmate and check each other's subject-verb agreement. Then tell a partner a new sentence that has a compound subject and uses correct subject-verb agreement.**

TEKS 4.20C
ELPS 2C, 4C, 5D

Subject-Verb Agreement 3

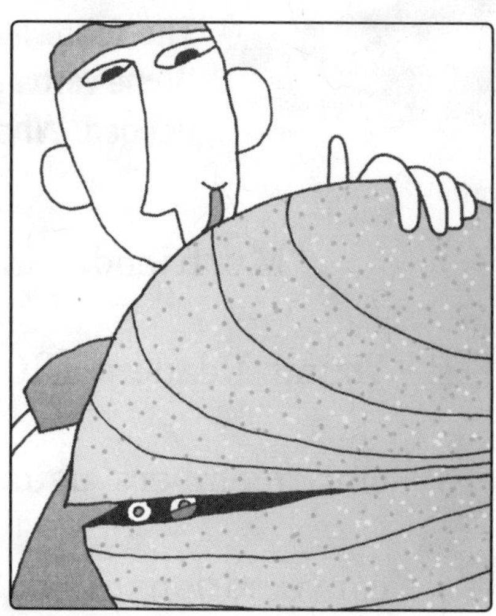

Subjects and verbs must also "agree" in compound sentences. Remember that a subject and a verb work together as a pair. Look for each pair in a compound sentence. (You should find two or more pairs.) Then make sure that each verb agrees with its subject. (See *Write Source* page 483.)

Example

I love books, and stories about space are my favorites.

In each of the compound sentences below, only one verb agrees with its subject. Cross out the incorrect verb and write the correct one above it. The verb you choose should agree with the subject. The first sentence has been done for you.

1. Hakim ~~visit~~ *visits* the library often, and he shows me some of his latest choices.

2. He loves books about animals, but some movies about animals also was on his desk.

3. Some movies give facts about animals; other films tells stories with animal characters.

4. That movie and this book talks about life in the ocean, and they look interesting to me.

5. I am borrowing the movie tonight, and this weekend Hakim and I am planning a trip to the library.

The following paragraphs have a mix of simple and compound sentences. Some verbs agree with their subjects; others do not. Correct the verbs where needed. When you are finished, each verb should agree with its subject.

My friends and I meet every Thursday. We ~~belongs~~ *belong* to the Young Readers Club, and our meetings are all about books. The club members usually begins each meeting seriously, but the conversations don't always stay that way. Sometimes Maria tell a joke, or Ben and Caitlyn sings a funny song. They kid me about my space stories, but I doesn't mind; after all, they is my friends!

The kids at that table often creates stories, and we feel excited about their new one. The story features some animal astronauts. One of the characters are named Captain Zebra, and his ship and crew sails through space faster than the speed of light! I like the "space" idea, Hakim cheer for any animal story, and the other kids and I wants a copy of the finished tale!

Learning Language **Write three compound sentences about stories that you like. Underline each subject once and each verb twice. Check that the subjects and verbs agree in each part of your compound sentences. Then tell your partner a new compound sentence with correct subject-verb agreement.**

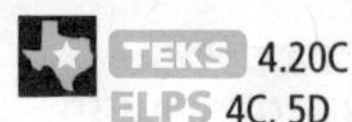
TEKS 4.20C
ELPS 4C, 5D

Subject-Verb Agreement Review

This activity gives you practice with subject-verb agreement.

Some of the underlined verbs below do not agree with their subjects. If the verb does not agree, cross it out and write the correct verb above it. If the verb does agree, put a check mark above it. The first two have been done for you.

My brother and sisters ~~is~~ *are* all teenagers. I ✓ have learned from them that teenagers is weird. For one thing, they does strange things to their hair. You never know what my sisters or my brother are going to do next. First, Kenny bleaches his hair; then he shave his head. When his hair starts to grow again, he look scary. Meanwhile, my sisters starts out with brown hair. They looks fine. Then one day Kelly have blonde hair, and Kendra have red hair. The next week, Kelly is a redhead, and Kendra are a blonde. Sometimes they even add stripes—blue, yellow, or red. My brother or my sisters is always in the bathroom doing things to their hair. Sometimes they tries to put things on my hair, and I have to scream for help. I tell my mom I are not going to be a teenager. She say, "That is okay with me. Your sisters and your brother is enough teenagers in one house."

In the sentences below, write the correct choice of the verbs shown in parentheses.

1. The whole class __________ to go on a field trip to Jacobsen's farm.
   (want, wants)

2. Students in the class __________ about getting too close to the animals.
   (worry, worries)

3. Janet and her two friends __________ they want to pat the horses.
   (say, says)

4. __________ the boys or the teacher going to sit close to the bus driver?
   (Is, Are)

5. The boys and the girls __________ that those in the back seats on the
   (agree, agrees)
   way to the farm will sit in the front seats on the way home.

6. The farmer or his sons __________ the gates every morning at 7:00 a.m.
   (open, opens)

7. Later in the day, the farmer's sons or his daughter __________ a calf.
   (rope, ropes)

8. During the visit, the farmer __________ a birdhouse for the students.
   (build, builds)

9. The teacher __________ Charlene and Sally to make a sign-up sheet.
   (ask, asks)

Learning Language **Write a simple sentence and a compound sentence. Underline each subject once and its verb twice. Check your subject-verb agreement. Then tell a partner a new simple sentence and a new compound sentence. Use correct subject-verb agreement. Have your partner identify the compound sentence and name the subjects and verbs.**

ELPS 4C, 5F

Combining Sentences Using Key Words

Too many short, choppy sentences make your writing . . . *rough!* To smooth it out and make it more fun to read, combine the short sentences using a key word or a series of words. (*Write Source* pages 484–485 tell you how.)

Example

Short Sentences:
At our school cafeteria, I like the lasagna.
I really like the burgers.
I like the fruit.

Combined Sentence:
At our school cafeteria, I like the lasagna, burgers, and fruit.

Combine each group of sentences to make one sentence. Use a key word or a series of words. The first one has been done for you.

1. Our school cafeteria is huge. Our school cafeteria is crowded. Our school cafeteria is noisy.

   Our school cafeteria is huge, crowded, and noisy.

2. You always have to wait in a line. The line is long.

   ____

   ____

3. You're supposed to wait for your turn. You're supposed to wait quietly.

   ____

   ____

ELPS 5F

4. The three lunch ladies are nice. They are helpful. They are busy.

5. We had a special dessert. We had it yesterday. It was made with apples and cinnamon.

6. We can choose a salad. We can choose pasta salad. We can choose lettuce salad. We can choose fruit salad.

7. The last school day before Thanksgiving, we have turkey. We also have dressing. We have pumpkin pie.

8. After lunch we help clean. We clean trays. We clean tables. We clean counters.

ELPS 4C, 5F

Combining Sentences with Phrases

There are many ways to combine sentences. (*Write Source* pages 484–485 tell more about how to combine sentences with phrases.)

Example

Two Sentences:
Jeff wants to become a professional baseball player. He is my brother's best friend.

Combined Sentence:
Jeff, my brother's best friend, wants to become a professional baseball player.

Practice combining sentences with prepositional phrases and appositive phrases. One example of each has been done for you. Notice how commas are used to set off appositive phrases. (See *Write Source* page 536.)

1. Mr. Gonzalez is a baseball player. He is our next-door neighbor.

   Mr. Gonzalez, our next-door neighbor, is a baseball player.

2. He signed his name. He signed it on a baseball.

   He signed his name on a baseball.

3. Mrs. Fowler asked him for his autograph. She is my teacher.

   ____

   ____

4. He plays the outfield. He plays for the Texas Drovers.

   ____

   ____

ELPS 4C, 5F

5. He gave me two free tickets. They are for the last home game of the season. That was right after he moved in.

6. He told me to come to the dugout. He told me to come before the game.

The Next Step **Write a paragraph about a favorite sport or pastime. Try to use several appositive and prepositional phrases. When you finish, circle them. Share your writing with a classmate.**

ELPS 4C

Sentence Combining with Compound Subjects and Predicates

You can combine sentences by using **compound subjects and predicates (verbs).** (See *Write Source* page 486. Also see pages 472 and 596–598 for more on compound subjects and predicates.)

Examples

Compound Subject:

Larry gave his speech today.
Maria gave her speech today.
Larry and Maria gave their speeches today.

Compound Predicate:

The teacher laughed. She dropped her book.
The teacher laughed and dropped her book.

Directions

Combine the pairs of sentences below using either a compound subject or a compound predicate. In parentheses, write "CS" if you used a compound subject and "CP" if you used a compound predicate. The first one has been done for you.

1. Tim knows a lot about computers. Nasim knows a lot about computers.

   Tim and Nasim know a lot about computers. (CS)

2. Linda made a bird feeder. She hung it in her backyard.

   ____

   ____

ELPS 4C, 5F

3. Tracy raked the leaves. He put them in bags.

4. Tron called for you. Patrick called for you, too.

5. My shoes got wet. My socks got wet, too.

6. I finished my homework. I helped Jamie with his.

7. We went to the library. We finished our research papers.

8. Diana wanted to go home. Reva wanted to go home, too.

The Next Step **Use "school" and "library" as a compound subject in a sentence. Then write a sentence using "ran" and "jumped" as a compound predicate. Finally, write a sentence using "Jan" and "Lane" as a compound subject and using "talked" and "laughed" as a compound predicate.**

ELPS 4C, 5F

Sentence Combining Review 1

It's time to review all the different ways you've learned to combine sentences.

Directions **Combine each set of sentences below into a longer, smoother sentence.**

1. The ancient Greeks thought Poseidon caused earthquakes. He was their sea god. (Use an appositive phrase.)

____

____

2. The Japanese said quakes were caused by a huge catfish. It lived under the earth. (Use a subordinate clause starting with *that.*)

____

____

3. Scientists discovered the true cause of earthquakes. They discovered it recently. (Use a key word.)

____

____

4. The earth's crust moves. Land masses bump together. (Use *and* to make a compound sentence.)

____

____

5. This causes shaking. It causes buckling. It causes cracking. (Use a series of words.)

____

6. Bears can predict earthquakes. Other animals can, too.
(Use a compound subject.)

7. Bears usually hibernate all winter. The bears in a Japanese zoo suddenly woke up before one earthquake.
(Make a compound sentence.)

8. They woke up early and began pacing. They paced around their cage.
(Use a prepositional phrase.)

The Next Step **Write two short sentences about earthquakes. Your sentences can be serious or silly. Trade papers with a partner and combine each other's sentences.**

ELPS 4C, 5F

Sentence Combining Review 2

Here's your chance to show off your sentence-combining skills.

Rewrite the following paragraph. Use what you have learned about sentence combining to make it read more smoothly. The first combination has been done for you.

Everyone knows that the oceans provide fish. They provide many other products, too. For example, oceans provide seaweed. The Japanese use seaweed in cooking. The Irish use seaweed in cooking, too. Seaweed is also used to make paint. It is used to make toothpaste. It is even used to make ice cream. Oceans provide salt. Salt is made from seawater—another name for ocean water. This is done in China. Oceans also provide coral. Coral is used to make jewelry. Coral is found in shallow water.

Everyone knows that the oceans provide fish, but they provide many other products, too.

ELPS 4C, 5F–G

Now try it again. Combine some of the sentences to make the following paragraph read more smoothly.

The seas are filled with fish. They are also swimming with stories. There are stories about dragons. The dragons have two heads. There are tales about pirates. There are tales about sunken treasure. There are tales about ghost ships. One ghost ship was named the *Mary Celeste.* All its passengers disappeared at sea. This happened in 1872. They were never found. Herman Melville wrote a sea story. It is famous. It is about Moby Dick. Moby Dick is a whale. He is huge.

The Next Step **Choose one of the following: (1) Write a few more smooth, interesting sentences to finish the paragraph above. (2) On your own paper, tell a sea story you know, or make one up!**

ELPS 4C, 5B

Kinds of Sentences

There are four kinds of sentences. **Declarative** sentences make statements. **Imperative** sentences give commands. **Exclamatory** sentences show strong emotion. **Interrogative** sentences ask questions. (See *Write Source* page 479.)

Examples

Declarative: The eel is slippery.

Imperative: Don't feed the fish.

Exclamatory: Look at that barracuda's teeth!

Interrogative: Do you think all sharks are dangerous?

Write four sentences (one of each kind) about a favorite animal. Use the examples above as models.

Declarative:

____

____

Imperative:

____

____

Exclamatory:

____

____

Interrogative:

____

____

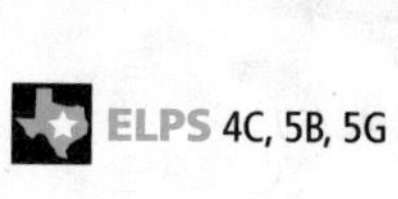

ELPS 4C, 5B, 5G

Directions **Read each of the sentences below and tell what kind of sentence it is. The first one has been done for you.**

Interrogative 1. Do all starfish have five arms?

_____________ 2. Actually, there are some that have as many as 20 arms.

_____________ 3. What is that starfish called?

_____________ 4. One name for it is the sunflower star.

_____________ 5. Look at that orange star near the shore.

_____________ 6. May I pick it up?

_____________ 7. No, do not disturb the animals in this area.

_____________ 8. Watch out for that large wave!

_____________ 9. If a seastar breaks off an arm, will the arm grow back?

_____________ 10. Starfish are able to regrow damaged arms.

_____________ 11. In fact, starfish can recover even if they are cut in two parts.

_____________ 12. I don't believe that!

_____________ 13. Well, it's true.

_____________ 14. How can a starfish do that?

_____________ 15. To be honest, no one really knows.

The Next Step **Exchange sentences from the previous page with a partner. Check to see that your classmate has written an example of each kind of sentence. Then write a paragraph about your favorite animal.**

ELPS 4C, 5B, 5F–G

Types of Sentences

Write Source pages 480–482 explain the three types of sentences: **simple sentences, compound sentences,** and **complex sentences.**

Examples

Simple Sentence:
My beaded necklace broke.

Compound Sentence:
I picked up the beads, and Kelly restrung them.

Complex Sentence:
Kelly will restring the beads if I find stronger string.

Next to each sentence below, write *simple, compound,* or *complex*. The first sentence has been done for you.

simple 1. Tomorrow I am going to start my book report.

________ 2. My best friend takes piano lessons because his parents think drums are too noisy.

________ 3. The gym teacher is strict, organized, and fair.

________ 4. My puppy has hair hanging down over her eyes, and she looks just like a dust mop.

________ 5. Our dog likes to eat shoes, but he won't touch my brother's smelly slippers.

________ 6. Tom and Mary danced around the room.

________ 7. The dog was friendly, playful, and smart.

The Next Step **Write three sentences about gym class. One sentence should be simple, one should be complex, and one should be compound.**

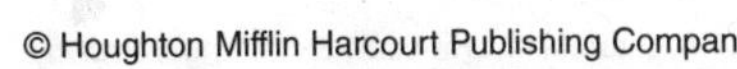

Change the following sentences to the type of sentence shown in parentheses. The first one has been done for you.

1. I know a lot about my state's capitol. I live near it. *(complex)*

   I know a lot about my state's capitol because I live near it.

2. I have lived in Lansing, Michigan my whole life. It is a great place to live. *(compound)*

3. The capitol is educational. The capitol is fun. *(simple)*

4. It has been restored. It has been rededicated. *(simple)*

5. The restoration was very expensive. Now the capitol is more interesting. *(compound)*

6. I go to the capitol. I look at the historical paintings in the building's dome. *(complex)*

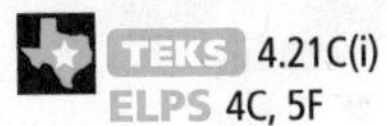
TEKS 4.21C(i)
ELPS 4C, 5F

Compound Sentences 1

You can combine sentences by making **compound sentences.** (See *Write Source* page 481.)

Example

Two Sentences:
John told us about his vacation.
It was scary.

Combined Sentence:
John told us about his vacation, and it was scary.

Combine each pair of sentences below into one compound sentence. Use a comma and a coordinating conjunction: *and, but, or, so, for, yet,* and *nor*.

1. John went hiking with his mother. He nearly stepped on a rattlesnake!

___

___

2. John knew he should back up slowly. He wanted to run.

___

___

3. John stayed cool. He slowly stepped away from the snake.

___

___

4. John says he's never going hiking again. His mom says he is kidding.

___

___

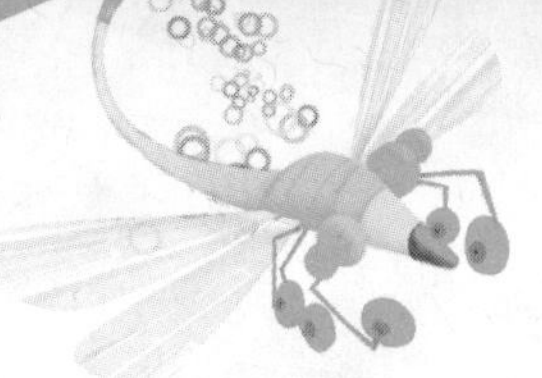

5. John's dad showed him pictures of snakes. John pointed to one of the pictures.

____

____

6. The snake he saw was a diamondback rattlesnake. He started to shake a little.

____

____

7. John's dad told him that snakes do not hunt people. Snakes do not want to bite people.

____

____

8. Hiking in the desert is fun. A hiker must walk carefully.

____

____

9. John had his camera and pack ready. He and his dad went hiking early the next day.

____

____

The Next Step **Jot down four simple sentences about an animal. Then exchange your work with a classmate. Combine each other's ideas into compound sentences. Be sure to use commas and conjunctions correctly.**

ELPS 4C, 5F

Compound Sentences 2

You can practice using coordinating conjunctions to form compound sentences.

For the sentences that follow, pick the best coordinating conjunction (*and, but, or, so, nor,* or *yet*) to complete each compound sentence. The first one has been done for you.

1. Malcom hit the ball, ___*and*___ it rolled into a street drain.
2. The boys looked into the drain, __________ the ball was out of reach.
3. They had to get the ball out of the drain, __________ the game was over.
4. Latrell had the longest arms, __________ he reached for the ball.
5. He couldn't grab it, __________ could he even touch it.
6. The boys looked for a stick, __________ none were long enough.
7. A policeman came by, __________ he asked them what they were doing.
8. They hoped he could help, __________ they told him what had happened.
9. The drain area was muddy, __________ he reached into the drain.
10. The policeman grabbed the ball, __________ the boys let out a cheer.
11. He gave them the baseball, __________ they thanked him.
12. The boys were ready to play again, __________ suddenly it started to rain.

TEKS 4.21C(i)
ELPS 4C, 5F

In the following paragraphs, join the short sentences with a conjunction from the list below. Place commas where needed and change capitalized letters. The first one has been done for you.

and but so or nor yet

In the United States, there are two very popular types of fruit. They are apples and oranges. Some people only like to eat apples. Other people only want oranges. Lots of apples are bright red. Some apples are green. Many people who like red apples don't like green ones.

More than 2,500 apple varieties are grown in the United States. More than 7,500 apple varieties are grown throughout the world. People can limit themselves to just one kind of apple. They can eat many kinds of apples. I don't like sour apples. I don't like mushy apples.

Many people think that all the oranges in this country are grown in Florida. Oranges are also grown in California. Some oranges are very easy to peel. People don't need a knife to eat them. Many oranges need to be cut into sections. Then they can be eaten easily. All oranges have vitamin C in them. Eating oranges is a good idea. Oranges can be eaten. They can be squeezed to make juice. Doctors say that eating apples and oranges is good for people. Eat an apple a day. Eat an orange a day instead.

The Next Step **Write four compound sentences about your favorite fruit. Use commas and these conjunctions in your sentences: *and, but, or, so.***

ELPS 4C, 5F

Complex Sentences 1

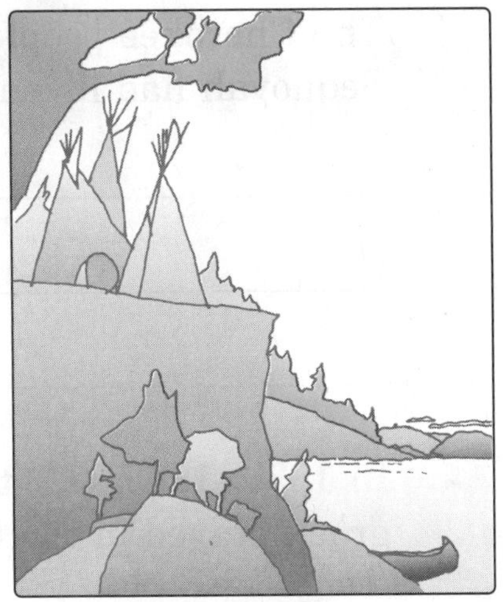

You can combine sentences to make complex sentences with one independent clause and one or more subordinate clauses. Often the subordinate clause starts with a **subordinating conjunction** (*although, because, if, since,* and so on). (See *Write Source* page 634 and "Write Complex Sentences" on *Write Source* page 482.)

Example

Two Sentences:
Many Native American tribes consisted of 1,500 to 3,000 people. The Cherokee numbered more than 50,000.

Combined Sentence:
Many Native American tribes consisted of only 1,500 to 3,000 people while the Cherokee nation numbered more than 50,000.

Combine each pair of sentences below to make one complex sentence. Use the conjunction in parentheses.

1. The Cherokee lived in the Appalachian Mountains. The tribe was the most powerful group in the area. **(where)**

____

____

2. A Cherokee named Sequoyah wanted to contact his friends. He did not know how to write. **(although)**

____

____

3. Sequoyah formed a symbol for each Cherokee sound. He had an alphabet of 86 letters. **(until)**

____

____

4. The Cherokee people were able to write in their own language. Sequoyah had invented an alphabet meant for them. **(because)**

5. In 1838–1839, U.S. troops moved the Cherokee to Oklahoma. A small group stayed in the Great Smoky Mountains. **(though)**

6. The winter march was called the Trail of Tears. Many Cherokee died on that trip. **(because)**

The Next Step **Write five sentences about a time you traveled someplace near or far. Use a different subordinating conjunction from the following list in each of your sentences:** ***after, although, because, before, if, since, though, unless, until, when, where, while.***

ELPS 4C, 5F

Complex Sentences 2

Two independent clauses can sometimes be combined into a complex sentence with a **relative pronoun** such as *who, whose, which,* or *that.* (*Write Source* page 614 explains these special pronouns.)

Example

Two Sentences:
Creek Indians lived in the eastern woodlands. Their neighbors were the Chickasaw and Yamasee tribes.

Combined Sentence:
Creek Indians, whose neighbors were the Chickasaw and Yamasee tribes, lived in the eastern woodlands.

Combine each pair of sentences below to make one complex sentence. Use the connecting word in parentheses.

1. They built more than 200 villages. Villages had 30 to 60 log houses each. **(which)**

____

____

2. The Creek lived in what is now Georgia and Alabama. They were farmers. **(who)**

____

____

3. The Creek lived in villages. The villages had central plazas. **(that)**

____

ELPS 4C, 5F

4. The central plaza had a rotunda. The rotunda was round and used for council meetings. **(which)**

5. Each town was governed by a chief. He made decisions for the people. **(who)**

6. The chief had an assistant. His job was to tell the people about the chief's decisions. **(whose)**

7. The homes of the Creek Indians were huts. The huts were covered with wood or grass. **(that)**

The Next Step **Write a long sentence for each of the following relative pronouns: *who, whose, which,* and *that*.**

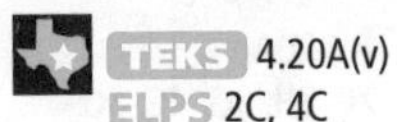
TEKS 4.20A(v)
ELPS 2C, 4C

Expanding Sentences with Prepositional Phrases

Prepositional phrases add details about a person, a place, a thing, or an idea. They tell location, time, or direction, and other details. (See *Write Source* page 487.)

Example

The boy threw the rock.

The boy in the blue shirt threw the rock across the creek.
(The prepositional phrase *in the blue shirt* tells which boy threw the rock. The phrase *across the creek* tells where the boy threw the rock.)

In the following sentences, underline each prepositional phrase and briefly explain what each phrase tells the reader (*What kind?, Which one?, Where?, When?, How?*). The first one has been done for you.

1. People of all ages love skipping rocks.
   what kind of people skip rocks

2. Flat rocks thrown fast enough can skip on the water's surface.
   ____

3. Both boys and girls shout with glee when a rock skips 20 times.
   ____

4. Some even lift their hands above their heads while they celebrate.
   ____

5. A rock skipper might not want to throw a rock after dark.
   ____

6. Rock skippers with a good arm can make 20 skips.
   ____

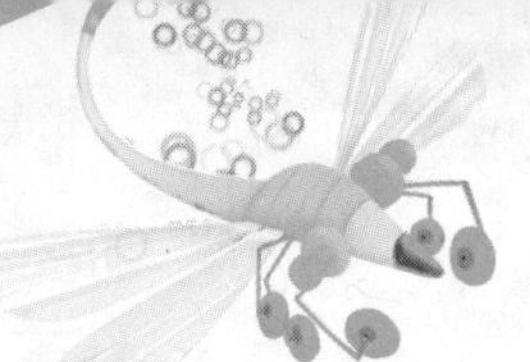

TEKS 4.20A(v)
ELPS 2C, 2H, 3G, 4C, 5G

Directions **Expand the following sentences by adding a prepositional phrase. Use the preposition shown in parentheses. Circle the prepositional phrase you add to the sentence. The first one has been done for you.**

1. The window is broken. **(in)**
   The window in my room is broken.

2. I am going. **(to)**
   ____

3. The sign has flashing neon lights. **(above)**
   ____

4. Jenny walked. **(out of)**
   ____

5. After a long search, Mr. Gregg found his keys. **(on top of)**
   ____

6. Robert could hear his cat purring. **(inside)**
   ____

7. Please find your assigned seat. **(at)**
   ____

8. Did I see you last night? **(near)**
   ____

Learning Language **Write several sentences using the prepositions *without, before, through,* and *against* to add information about location, time, direction, and other details. Then tell a partner two new sentences. Use a preposition in each.**

ELPS 4C, 5B

Sentence-Variety Review

This exercise reviews different types and kinds of sentences.

Identify the following sentences as "compound," "complex," or "simple." Also, list whether they are "declarative," "imperative," "interrogative," or "exclamatory." The first one has been done for you.

complex 1. Although water often looks blue, it is really colorless. *declarative*

______ 2. After you are seated, read this magazine article. ______

______ 3. Ricardo brought his science project into the room, and Ramon placed it near the window. ______

______ 4. One frog in the classroom's aquarium is green, but the other two frogs are brown with yellow streaks. ______

______ 5. That's a sharp knife! ______

______ 6. If you bring the right tools, you can finish the work today. ______

______ 7. You should hang your drawing on the wall, but you should not use masking tape. ______

______ 8. How many books did you read last summer? ______

______ 9. I found the missing football! ______

______ 10. Don't paint the wall with that old brush. ______

Combine or expand the sentences below according to the directions shown in parentheses. Make sure you include the right punctuation and change capitalization if necessary.

1. Paul carefully counted all the baseballs. Three baseballs were lost during practice. **(complex, use *although*)**

2. The coach thinks he saw a baseball. **(expand, use *under*)**

3. Waylan remembers seeing one baseball near the fence. Drake says he saw one by the dugout. **(compound, use *while*)**

4. Barry stopped looking. It was getting dark. **(complex, use *because*)**

5. Paul hopes to find the three missing baseballs. The coach will have to buy new ones. **(compound, use *or*)**

Language Activities

Every activity in this section includes a main practice part in which you learn about or review the different parts of speech. Most of the activities also include helpful references in the Student Edition of *Texas Write Source*. In addition, Learning Language, which is at the end of most activities, encourages follow-up practice of certain skills.

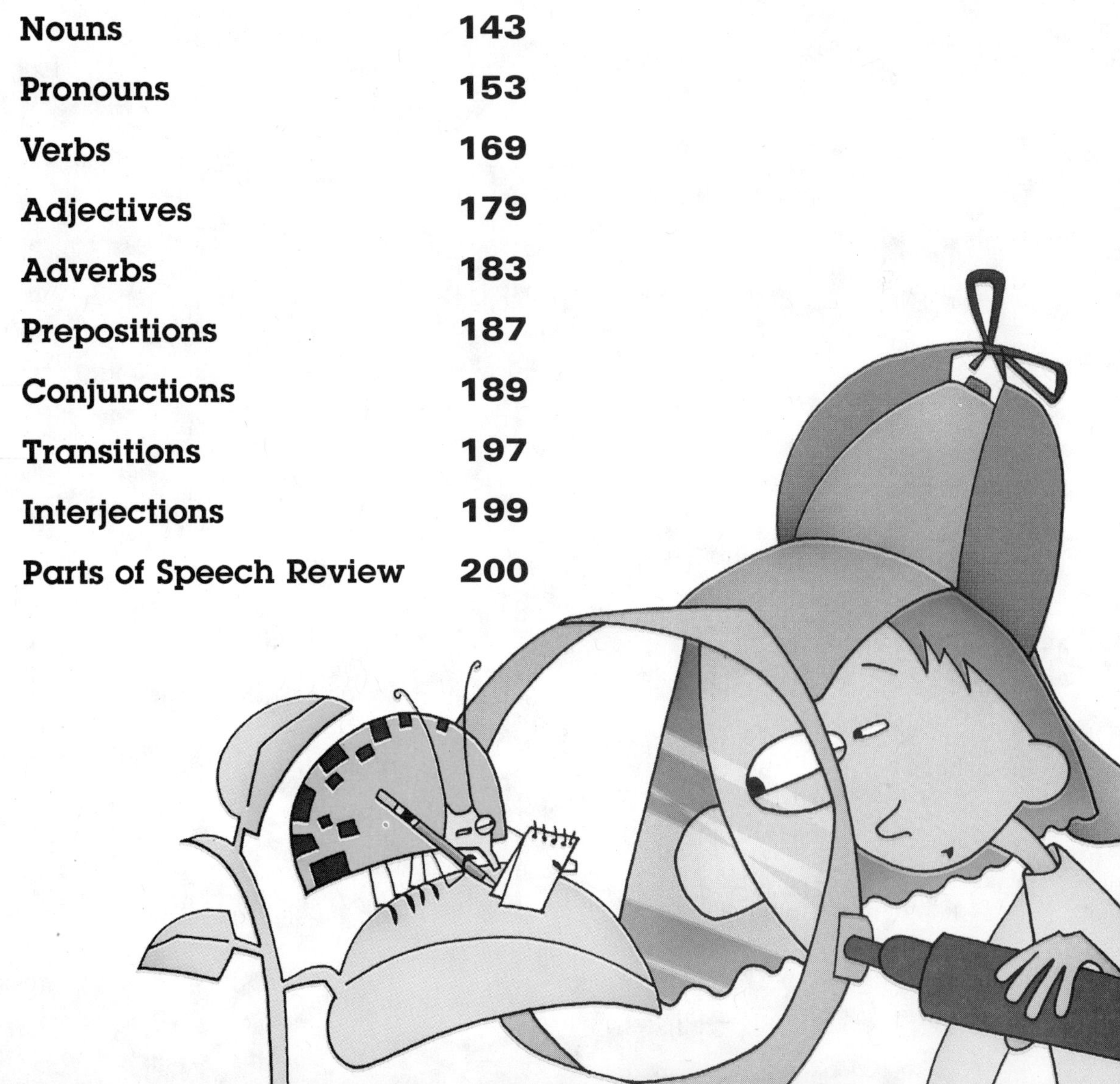

ELPS 2C, 4C

Nouns

A **noun** names a person, a place, a thing, or an idea. (See *Write Source* page 604.)

Examples

A Person: aquanaut

A Place: Mariana Trench

A Thing: ocean

An Idea: oceanography

Circle all the nouns in the sentences below. The number after each sentence tells you how many nouns it has. The first sentence has been done for you.

1. I was so surprised you could have knocked me over with a feather. *(1)*
2. Don't sit there like a bump on a log. *(2)*
3. That boy is barking up the wrong tree. *(2)*
4. It's all water under the bridge. *(2)*
5. Rome wasn't built in a day. *(2)*
6. The doctors x-rayed my head and found nothing wrong. *(3)*
7. This is the greatest city in America. *(2)*
8. Forgetfulness is my biggest weakness. *(2)*
9. Don't miss tomorrow's game. *(1)*
10. Let's hope Steve gets his curveball working. *(2)*

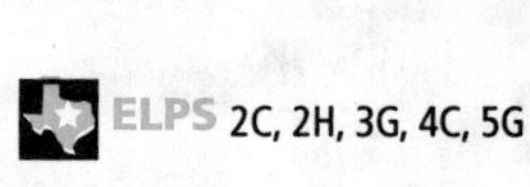

ELPS 2C, 2H, 3G, 4C, 5G

Directions **In the sentences below, circle the nouns and label each noun as "person," "place," "thing," or "idea." The first one has been done for you.**

1. The Atlantic Ocean (place) is the body of water between North America and Europe.
2. A scuba diver may explore ancient shipwrecks.
3. Fear keeps some people out of the water.
4. Great white sharks can be almost 30 feet long.
5. Jacques Cousteau invented the aqualung for breathing underwater.
6. Some of his friends sailed on *Calypso* with him around the world.
7. There are some dangers involved in scuba dives.
8. Deep water has a colder temperature than surface water.
9. A swimmer sometimes uses a snorkel and a mask.
10. Some people prefer a nice, warm swimming pool.

Learning Language **Write four sentences about your school. Circle and identify all of the nouns. Then tell a partner a sentence that uses three nouns: one to name a person, one to name a place, and one to name a thing.**

TEKS 4.20A(ii)
ELPS 2C, 2G–I, 3D–E, 4C

Common and Proper Nouns

A **common noun** is the *general* name of a person, a place, a thing, or an idea. A **proper noun** is a *particular* name of a person, a place, a thing, or an idea. Remember to capitalize proper nouns. (See *Write Source* page 604.)

Examples

Common Nouns: man, woman

Proper Nouns: Mr. Thun, Ms. Felipe

Write a common noun to go with each proper noun. Then write a proper noun to go with each common noun.

Proper Nouns	Common Nouns
1. Amarillo	____________
2. Florida	____________
3. Pacific	____________
4. Sunday	____________
5. ____________	boy
6. ____________	school
7. ____________	team

Learning Language **Write a few sentences about a place you would like to visit. Use common and proper nouns. Identify each noun as common or proper by writing a "C" or "P" above it. Then use common and proper nouns to tell a partner two new sentences about your school. Discuss whether each noun is common or proper.**

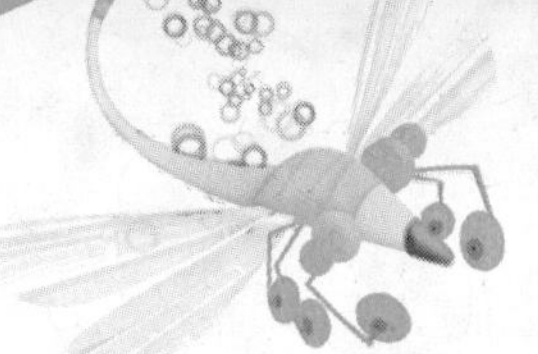

Concrete and Abstract Nouns

Concrete nouns name things that can be touched or seen. **Abstract nouns** name things that cannot be touched or seen. (See *Write Source* page 604.)

Examples

Concrete Nouns: shoe, building, sky, Ohio

Abstract Nouns: mystery, laziness, fear

Sort the nouns below into two groups: concrete and abstract nouns. Write each noun in the correct column.

tractor	idea	supermarket	sun
students	strength	hope	sadness
zoo	health	thought	lawn

Concrete Nouns	Abstract Nouns
______________	______________
______________	______________
______________	______________
______________	______________
______________	______________
______________	______________

Learning Language Now think of three more nouns to add to each column. If you need ideas, look around you! Things you can see are concrete nouns. Moods, feelings, ideas, and so on, are abstract nouns. Then use concrete and abstract nouns to tell a partner two new sentences.

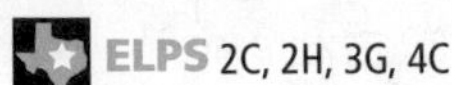
ELPS 2C, 2H, 3G, 4C

Compound Nouns

Two or more words make up a **compound noun**. Compound nouns can add interest to your writing.

Examples

flashlight *(written as one word)*
picture tube *(written as two words)*
sister-in-law *(written with hyphens)*

Choose from the list of compound nouns below to replace the underlined noun in each sentence below. The first one has been done for you.

rainbow	firefighter	president-elect
house cat	forklift	fullback
blue jeans	babysitter	fish fry

1. The ~~man~~ firefighter sprayed water on the burning building.
2. The warehouse worker used a machine to move the heavy crate.
3. Our runner carried the ball over the goal line for our first touchdown.
4. I saw their friendly animal curled up in a sunny spot.
5. Randy likes his comfortable pants.
6. Mom and Dad have called a person to stay with my little sister tonight.
7. The politician moves into the White House in January.
8. Bill likes the trout served at the annual picnic.
9. After the rain, Jeff looked for the sight in the sky.

Learning Language **Use a dictionary to find three other compound nouns. Write a sentence for each noun. Then tell a partner a sentence that uses another compound noun.**

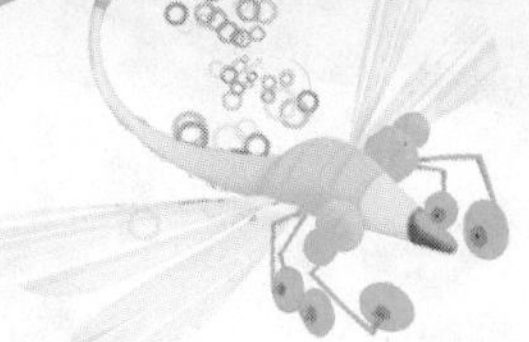

Number and Gender of Nouns

A noun that names only one person, place, thing, or idea is singular. If it names more than one, it is plural. A noun is feminine if it refers to a female and masculine if it refers to a male. A neuter noun refers to an object that is neither male nor female. An indefinite noun could be either male or female. (See *Write Source* page 606.)

Examples

Number		***Gender***	
Singular Nouns:	shoe, student	*Masculine:*	boy, son, nephew, bull
Plural Nouns:	shoes, students	*Feminine:*	girl, daughter, niece, cow
		Neuter:	nail, pencil, paper, shoe
		Indefinite:	child, parent, student, deer

Directions **Identify the following nouns. The first one has been done for you.**

singular, neuter	1. car	______	11. sister
______	2. house	______	12. hen
______	3. librarian	______	13. books
______	4. nephew	______	14. daughter
______	5. birds	______	15. ladies
______	6. aunt	______	16. uncle
______	7. bucket	______	17. cow
______	8. scouts	______	18. rock
______	9. coyotes	______	19. bee
______	10. men	______	20. actresses

Learning Language **Choose two plural and two singular nouns. Write a sentence with each. Then tell a partner sentences that use masculine, feminine, neuter, and indefinite nouns.**

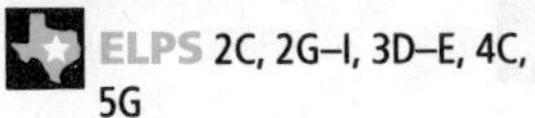
ELPS 2C, 2G–I, 3D–E, 4C, 5G

Uses of Nouns 1

In the following sentences, underline the subject noun and circle the predicate noun. Some sentences may have both a subject noun and a predicate noun. The first one has been done for you. (See *Write Source* page 608.)

1. Starlings are not native birds in the United States.
2. More than 100 years ago, a group of people brought starlings from England.
3. Many people enjoyed the metallic-colored birds.
4. Those bird lovers were surprised that starlings multiplied so quickly.
5. Aggressive starlings often drive away other birds.
6. These birds can be seen as pests.
7. The English sparrow is an import.
8. This plain brown bird can be found throughout the United States.
9. English sparrows are another problem.
10. The bird's nest is a messy place.
11. A flock of these sparrows often crowd out other birds.
12. Perhaps people should not import foreign birds and animals.

Learning Language **Write a sentence about a bird that uses a subject noun and a predicate noun. Then tell a partner a new sentence that uses a subject noun and a predicate noun. Discuss the difference between a predicate noun and an object noun. (See *Write Source* page 608.)**

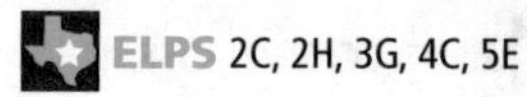

Uses of Nouns 2

Possessive nouns show ownership. (See *Write Source* page 608 for an explanation of possessives.) Add an *-'s* for most singular nouns and an apostrophe after the *s* for most plurals. Some plurals need an *-'s*.

Examples

The girl's lunch was left on the bus. *("girl," a singular noun)*

The girls' picnic was delayed by rain. *("girls," a plural noun)*

The men's volleyball tournament is next week. *("men," a plural noun)*

Fill each blank in the following sentences with the correct possessive form of the noun shown in parentheses. The first one has been done for you.

1. A ___tree's___ leaves release oxygen into the air. *(tree)*

2. The class spent an hour looking for ________________ book. *(Dan)*

3. This is the last game for the ________________ soccer team. *(boys)*

4. Did you find our ________________ collar in the park? *(dog)*

5. The ________________ mother will pick them up at noon. *(children)*

6. I didn't like that ________________ cover. *(book)*

7. The ________________ winds grew stronger every hour. *(hurricane)*

8. In our solar system, none of the ________________ orbits are the same. *(planets)*

Learning Language **Rewrite one of the sentences above to make the singular possessive noun plural. (*Example:* Trees' leaves release oxygen into the air.) Rewrite another to make the plural possessive noun singular. Then tell a partner a new sentence that uses a possessive noun.**

ELPS 4C, 5B

Nouns as Objects 1

When you think of nouns, you probably think of them as the subjects of sentences. But nouns may also be used as **objects**. In the two sentences below, *dog* and *street* are objects. (*Write Source* page 608 explains nouns used as objects.)

Examples

The cat chased the dog.

(The word *dog* is a direct object.)

The ball rolled into the street.

(The word *street* is the object of the preposition *into.)*

Each sentence below has at least one noun used as an object. Underline and label each object: "direct object," "indirect object," or "object of preposition." The first one has been done for you.

indirect object *direct object*

1. The teacher gave Julie a pencil.
2. Mom parked behind the school.
3. Joey called the police.
4. We built a playhouse in our backyard.
5. Mom painted our house.
6. Last night, I read Brad a story.
7. Rene gave Michael a cookie.
8. Darla sent the teacher a valentine.
9. Gerardo gave a speech to our class.

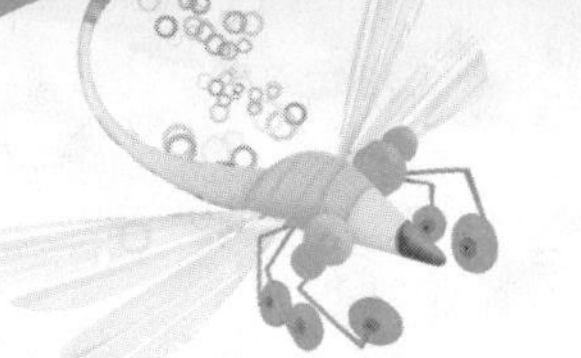

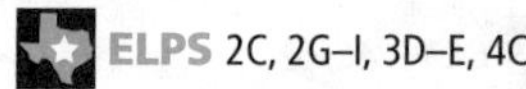

ELPS 2C, 2G–I, 3D–E, 4C

Nouns as Objects 2

This page gives you more practice recognizing objects.

Directions **In the paragraph below, circle the indirect objects, underline the direct objects, and underline the objects of prepositions twice. The first sentence has been done for you. (See *Write Source* page 608.)**

Mosquitoes bother people in the summer. These insects bite people more often during hot, muggy weather. Mosquitoes can make an animal's life miserable. Some people swat the mosquitoes. Sometimes mosquito bites aren't noticed. Later, those bites cause the skin to swell. Then people may scratch the itchy bumps. Scratched bumps only feel itchier. A mosquito bite can give an allergic person a huge bump. On hot nights, a mosquito's noisy wings can even keep adults awake. Most mosquito bites don't cause trouble. Some mosquitoes can give people diseases. Parents can buy insect sprays and creams for the whole family. Adults give children mosquito repellent. Some of these products even keep mosquitoes off the skin. Swarms of insects can ruin a nice summer day.

Learning Language **Tell a partner a sentence that uses a direct object and an indirect object. Discuss which object is which. Then tell your partner another sentence that uses the object of a preposition.**

ELPS 2C, 4C

Person of a Pronoun

The **person of a pronoun** tells you whether the pronoun represents the person who is speaking, the person who is being spoken to, or the person or thing that is being spoken about. (See *Write Source* page 610.)

Examples

	First-Person Pronoun	Second-Person Pronoun	Third-Person Pronoun
	Stands for Person Speaking	Stands for Person Being Spoken To	Stands for Person or Thing Being Spoken About
Singular	**I**	**you**	**he, she, it**
Plural	**we**	**you**	**they**

In the sentences below, fill in each blank with the correct pronoun from the table above. The first one has been done for you.

____*I*____ have a friend named Jerry who went out on a boat to see whales in the ocean. __________ have to come to the surface to breathe. Jerry said __________ saw four whales. __________ said __________ slap their tails on the water, just for fun. __________ said that one whale was so close to the boat that when __________ slapped its tail, water splashed on him.

A whale expert named Tasha was on the boat. __________ told Jerry that whales eat one ton of food every day. __________ told Jerry I didn't believe it. __________ answered, "If __________ saw how big __________ are, you'd believe it!"

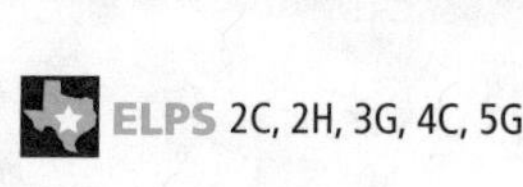

ELPS 2C, 2H, 3G, 4C, 5G

Directions **In the following sentences, the personal pronouns are underlined. Write a "1" above each first-person pronoun, a "2" above each second-person pronoun, and a "3" above each third-person pronoun. The first sentence has been done for you.**

1. He likes me, and I like him. (3, 1, 1, 3)
2. Do you want to go sledding with me?
3. We had hot cocoa, and they built a snowman.
4. They put a hat on its head.
5. Where did you and he go?
6. Is she going with you or with me?
7. You and I should go in their car.
8. They don't know where his house is.
9. She borrowed the sled from him because he wasn't using it.
10. You can return it to us or to them.
11. Is our sled in your car or in their car?
12. We could put our toboggan on the roof of the van if it fits.

Learning Language **Write three sentences about an activity you like to do. Use first-person, second-person, and third-person pronouns. Then tell a partner a new sentence using first-person and second-person pronouns.**

ELPS 4C

Number of a Pronoun 1

A **pronoun** can be either singular or plural. (See *Write Source* page 610.)

Examples

Singular

Bob went to the store.	He went to the store.

(The singular pronoun *He* replaces the singular noun *Bob.)*

Plural

The girls are hungry.	They are hungry.

(The plural pronoun *They* replaces the plural noun *girls.)*

Label the underlined pronouns in the sentences below with "S" for singular or "P" for plural. Draw an arrow to the noun the pronoun replaces. The first one has been done for you.

S S

1. Sheila looked for the blue hat, but she could not find it.
2. The wind was strong, and it was cold.
3. Sheila's brother, Dave, gave her a hat.
4. Although Sheila and Dave were cold, they kept walking.
5. Mrs. Smith said to Sheila and Dave, "You look cold."
6. Mrs. Smith decided she would give the two walkers some hot cider.
7. Sheila and Dave said to Mrs. Smith, "Thank you for the hot cider."
8. Both Sheila and Dave said they were glad to get warm again.

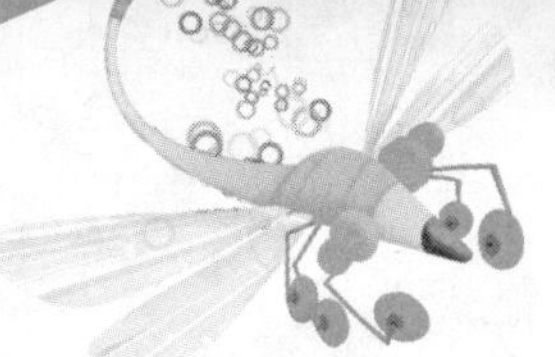

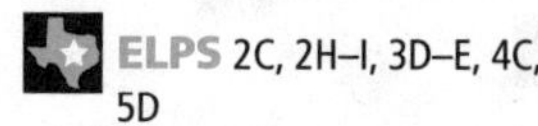

ELPS 2C, 2H–I, 3D–E, 4C, 5D

Number of a Pronoun 2

Read the following paragraphs and replace the underlined words with the correct pronouns. The first one has been done for you.

My dad thought I would like a model spaceship for my birthday, so ~~Dad~~ *he* bought a space shuttle. The shuttle was made of plastic, but some parts were metal. I was excited because the model was so detailed. Of course, my dad wanted to help me, so Dad and I worked together on the model. Mom and my sister liked watching us work, so Mom and my sister would check on Dad and me sometimes. My best friend, Joe, stopped by to help, too. My dad, Joe, and I each worked on different parts of the shuttle. Then, we assembled the three parts. Once the whole model was together, we set the model aside to let the glue dry.

I talked to the man who owns the hobby shop, and the hobby shop owner told me to use spray enamel. The hobby shop owner said the spray would look better than painting by hand. We decided to paint the shuttle in the garage.

Learning Language **Write three sentences that use singular and plural pronouns. Then tell a partner a sentence that uses singular and plural nouns. Ask your partner to say the sentence back to you using pronouns instead of nouns.**

ELPS 4C

Subject and Object Pronouns 1

A **pronoun** is a word used in place of a noun. A **subject pronoun** is used as the subject of a sentence. An **object pronoun** is used after an action verb or in a prepositional phrase. (See *Write Source* page 612.)

Examples

Subject Pronoun: We got lost.

Object Pronoun: Mom and Dad found us.

Each sentence below contains a subject pronoun, an object pronoun, or both. Underline each pronoun. Write "S" above each subject pronoun and "O" above each object pronoun. The first sentence has been done for you.

1. We (S) found them (O) in the library.
2. I left it at school.
3. We helped her find the books.
4. She needed them.
5. After dessert, he read me a story.
6. You saw us at the mall.
7. He got a new sweater.
8. It fits him.
9. Yesterday, Paulo wrote me a note.
10. The teacher saw it.

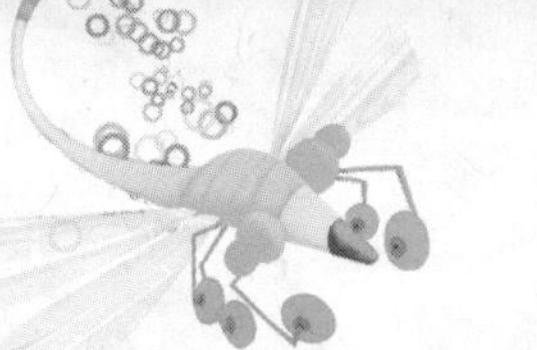

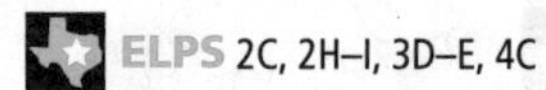

Cross out the complete subject in each sentence below. Replace the subject with the correct subject pronoun: *he, she, it,* or *they.* The first one has been done for you.

1. ~~Philip~~ *He* likes bananas.
2. Jessica brought the cake.
3. The weather is too cold for Harry.
4. Tim and Charlie know Michelle.
5. Last night, my parents met my teacher and her husband.
6. The house belongs to Ms. Rojas.
7. After school, Jeff walked home with Sue.
8. The cat belongs to Juanita.
9. Elena found the book for Jose.
10. Mr. Montoya listened to the band students practice.
11. The close game got the fans excited.
12. Erika and Laura wrapped the present.
13. Michelle forgot to call her parents.
14. John ate the hot fudge sundae.
15. Six students helped decorate the stage.

Learning Language **Now cross out each object noun or noun phrase in the above sentences. Write the correct object pronoun (*him, her, it,* or *them*) above it. Then tell a partner a sentence that uses a subject noun and an object noun. (*Hint*: Use an action verb.) Ask your partner to say the sentence back to you with pronouns instead of nouns.**

ELPS 2C, 4C

Subject and Object Pronouns 2

A **subject pronoun** is used as the subject of a sentence. An **object pronoun** is used after an action verb or in a prepositional phrase. A **possessive pronoun** shows ownership. (To learn more about each of these pronouns, carefully read the sample sentences and the information about personal pronouns on *Write Source* page 612.)

Circle the pronouns in the following sentences. Label the pronouns with "S" for subject, "O" for object, or "P" for possessive. Then go back and mark "Si" for singular or "Pl" for plural. The first one has been done for you.

1. He (S Si) walked with his (P Si) dog for two hours.
2. The dog tried to run, but Jeff stopped it with the leash.
3. Then, Jeff's friends asked him to go to a movie with them.
4. They went to see the newest movie at the theater.
5. They paid for their tickets and walked toward the popcorn machine.
6. A man stopped them and said, "Show me your tickets, please."
7. Nancy used some of her money to buy gum.
8. She joined the rest of the group just before the movie got started.
9. She almost missed its opening scene.
10. Jeff whispered, "Why were you so late?"
11. "I couldn't find the flavor of gum that I like," she answered.

Learning Language Write a paragraph about something your school is proud of. Trade paragraphs with a classmate and circle all of your partner's pronouns. Then put each pronoun into the correct box below. Return the papers and check each other's work. Then tell a partner two new sentences using subject and object pronouns to tell something you are proud of.

Subject Pronouns

Singular	
Plural	

Object Pronouns

Singular	
Plural	

Possessive Pronouns

Singular	
Plural	

 ELPS 4C

Possessive Pronouns

A **possessive pronoun** shows ownership. (See *Write Source* page 612.)

Examples

We wrote our poems on the board.
Mine was the shortest.
Yours was the funniest.

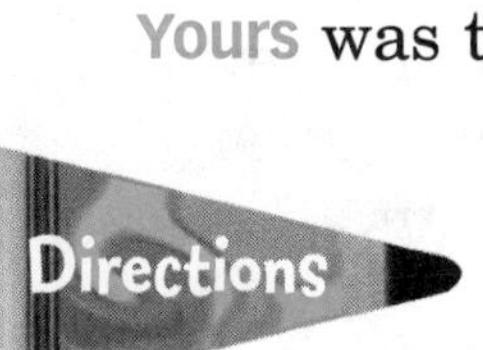

Underline the possessive pronouns in the following sentences. The first sentence has been done for you.

1. Our teacher read my poem.
2. The fifth graders had their field trip today.
3. The fourth grade has its field trip next week.
4. Which softball is ours, and which is theirs?
5. Did you bring your glove?
6. No, but Buddy brought his.
7. He brought his bats, too.
8. My brother is watching our jackets for us.
9. Is that my glass, or yours?
10. That's her glass; this one is yours.
11. I thought the other one was hers!
12. The one that's full is mine.

ELPS 2H, 3G, 4C

Learning Language **Replace each underlined word or phrase below with a possessive pronoun. The first one has been done for you. Then use possessive pronouns to tell a partner two sentences about your favorite thing.**

his

One the way to school, Jeremy dropped Jeremy's backpack in a big puddle of slush. All of Jeremy's books, papers, markers, and everything else got soaked. When the teacher collected homework, Jeremy handed Jeremy's homework in—still dripping! When Jeremy needed a pen, he asked Alicia if he could borrow Alicia's pen. Of course, he needed paper, too, so he asked Mark for some of Mark's paper. When he needed a dry math book, he asked me if he could share my math book. At lunch, Jeremy needed dry food! Hannah and Todd let Jeremy share Hannah's and Todd's sandwiches. Tina and I told Jeremy that if he wanted some raw carrots, he could have our raw carrots.

Jeremy said, "Thanks, Jim, but I'd rather eat Jeremy's wet cookies than Tina's and Jim's dry carrots."

Tina gave some of Tina's dessert to Jeremy. I gave him a banana and said, "Sorry, buddy, but this brownie is all my brownie!"

Reflexive Pronouns

A **reflexive pronoun** refers back to the subject of a sentence. Reflexive pronouns end with *-self* or *-selves*. (See *Write Source* pages 452 and 614.)

Examples

We enjoyed ourselves at the costume shop.
Dan and Marcus tried on some cowboy outfits by themselves.
Marcus gave himself an A+ for his new look.

Underline the reflexive pronouns in the following sentences. The first sentence has been done for you.

1. We were choosing party costumes for ourselves that day.
2. Rachel talked to herself while looking at fancy dresses.
3. Then, she and Ana dressed themselves as princesses.
4. I said, "Ana, take a look at yourself in the mirror."
5. Ana saw herself in the royal costume and laughed.
6. "I could rule this country by myself!" she announced.
7. "You and Rachel should find yourselves another choice," Dan said.
8. I asked myself, "Which costume choice is best?"
9. Marcus said, "You might try imagining yourself at the party."
10. I did, and the right costume—a clown suit—revealed itself to me!
11. The store owner smiled to himself as we paid the rental fee.
12. We told ourselves that we would look great at the party.

Complete the following story. Fill in each blank with the correct reflexive pronoun. The first one has been done for you.

Dressed as a clown, I went by ___myself___ to the party. I saw Marcus when I got there. "You should congratulate ____________," I told him. "You look great!"

Then Ana came in—but in a spacesuit! "She gave ____________ a makeover," Marcus said. "Yes," Ana explained, "Rachel and I decided for ____________ that she should be the princess. I told ____________ that this was the right outfit for me."

Just then Mr. and Mrs. Evans, our hosts, came in and laughed to ____________. Mrs. Evans said, "You kids all have made ____________ look wonderful!" Mr. Evans took some pictures of us for ____________, his wife, and us.

The music was good by ____________, but the games were even better. The Evanses really outdid ____________!

Learning Language **Write five sentences about a costume you would wear to this party. Use a reflexive pronoun in each one. Then use reflexive pronouns to tell a partner about something you like to do when you are alone.**

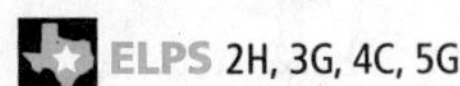
ELPS 2H, 3G, 4C, 5G

Indefinite Pronouns

An **indefinite pronoun** refers to things that are not named or are unknown. (See the bottom of *Write Source* page 614 for a list of indefinite pronouns.)

Examples

Several forgot their lunches.

Each of them bought a snack in the cafeteria.

Underline the indefinite pronouns in the following sentences. (Some sentences have more than one indefinite pronoun.)

1. Someone left all of these books here.
2. Some of us have finished our projects.
3. Most of us did all of our homework.
4. Everybody is going to the library.
5. In the end, everything turned out fine.
6. Both of my brothers are older than I am.
7. None of us remembered to bring anything to drink.
8. Each of us was supposed to bring something.

Learning Language **An indefinite pronoun is a bit mysterious; it does not name the word it replaces. Write five sentences that sound as if they were taken from a mystery story. Use at least one indefinite pronoun in each sentence. For example: *Suddenly, everyone was silent.* Then use an indefinite pronoun tell a partner a new sentence you could use in a mystery story.**

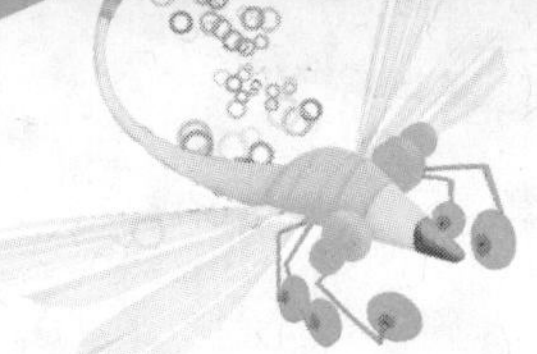

Demonstrative Pronouns

A **demonstrative pronoun** identifies a noun without naming it. The demonstrative pronouns are *this, that, these,* and *those*. *This* and *that* are singular. *These* and *those* are plural. *This* and *these* often point out something close or something new. *That* and *those* point out something far away or something older.

Examples

Have you seen Rafi's red pen? **This** must be it.

Directions **Fill in the blanks with "this," "that," "these," or "those" to complete the sentences below. The first one has been done for you.**

1. Are they still playing the game? Yes, _this_ is going to be a long one.
2. Look at Jorge's model car. He bought ________ yesterday.
3. I noticed the mess in the kitchen. Who did ________?
4. I tried on the wraparound glasses and said, " ________ are some of the strangest-looking sunglasses I have ever seen."
5. Hank held up two blue hats and asked, "Are ________ for sale?"
6. Look at the large painted carving on the table by the door. ________ is a very pleasing art project.
7. Talk to the players at the side of the field and tell ________ without helmets that they can't play.
8. Go look at Room 22. ________ is the way to paint the walls in Room 201.
9. Mr. Thompson held up Mark's paper and said, "________ is well done."

Learning Language **Write four sentences. Use one of the demonstrative pronouns in each one. Then use a demonstrative pronoun to tell a partner a sentence about a nearby object.**

ELPS 2C, 3D, 4C, 5D–E

Pronoun-Antecedent Agreement

The pronouns in your sentences must agree with their antecedents. An **antecedent** is the name for the noun that a pronoun replaces. (See *Write Source* page 453.)

Examples

Rod's sister lost her sunglasses at the beach.
(The pronoun *her* and the word it replaces, *sister,* are both singular, so they agree.)

Angie *and* Julie go body surfing whenever they can.
(The pronoun *they* and the words it replaces, *Angie and Julie,* are both plural, so they agree.)

Circle the pronouns in each of the following sentences. Draw an arrow to each pronoun's antecedent. If a pronoun does not agree with this antecedent, cross it out and write the correct pronoun above it. The first one has been done for you.

1. Rod and Angie got up early so ~~she~~ *they* could go on the tide-pool walk.
2. The naturalist told the group of early-morning hikers to follow them.
3. People wore rain gear because they were told to expect rain on the Olympic coast.
4. As the sun rose over the Olympic Mountains, they created a foggy, golden glow.
5. Rod slipped on the tide-pool rocks that had seaweed growing on it.
6. Tentacles coming from the sea anemones made it look like flowers to Angie.

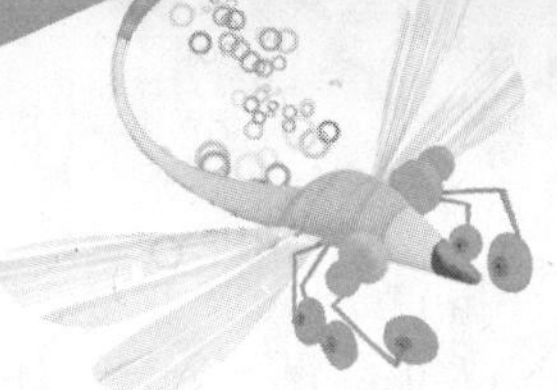

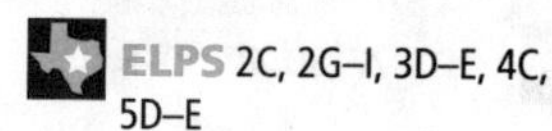

ELPS 2C, 2G–I, 3D–E, 4C, 5D–E

7. One deep-orange starfish lifted an arm as it moved across a rock in slow motion.

8. Empty sea urchin shells were scattered about where seagulls left them.

9. The yellow sea slugs crossing the pool looked like it needed a rest.

10. Angie liked barnacles that they thought looked like jumping jacks.

11. As the tide started coming in, Rod called for Angie to wait for him.

12. Then the tide pools disappeared; they will reappear at the next low tide.

Learning Language **Write two pairs of sentences. In the first sentence, use a noun. In the second sentence of each pair, use a pronoun that agrees with the antecedent in your first sentence. Then tell a partner a new sentence with a pronoun and an antecedent. Discuss how the pronoun and antecedent agree.**

1. ______________________________

____

2. ______________________________

____

1. ______________________________

____

2. ______________________________

____

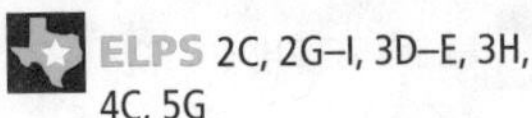
ELPS 2C, 2G–I, 3D–E, 3H, 4C, 5G

Types of Verbs 1

There are three types of **verbs**. (See *Write Source* page 616.) **Action verbs** tell what the subject is doing. **Linking verbs** link a subject to a noun or an adjective. **Helping verbs** help state an action or show time.

Examples

Action Verbs: ran, jumped
Linking Verbs: was, seemed
Helping Verbs: have, will

Directions

Write down as many examples of each type of verb as you can in 5 minutes! When your time is up, use the explanations in *Write Source* to check your verbs.

Action Verbs	Linking Verbs	Helping Verbs
______	______	______
______	______	______
______	______	______
______	______	______
______	______	______
______	______	______
______	______	______
______	______	______

Learning Language **Write a story about preparing and eating your favorite food. Underline and label the verbs in your story: "A" (action), "L" (linking), or "H" (helping). Discuss your answers with a partner. Then tell your partner a short story that uses action, linking, and helping verbs.**

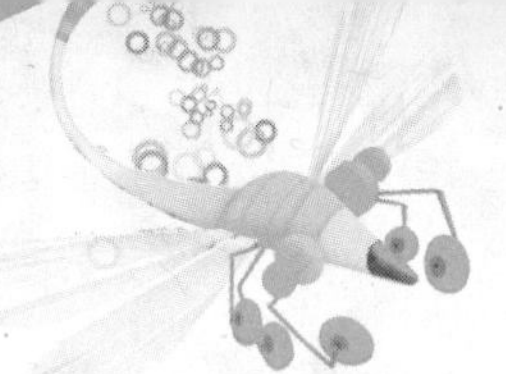

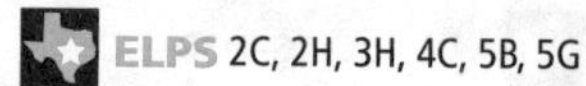
ELPS 2C, 2H, 3H, 4C, 5B, 5G

Types of Verbs 2

There are three types of verbs: action verbs, linking verbs, and helping verbs. (They're explained on *Write Source* page 616.)

Examples

Action Verbs: watch, swam

Linking Verbs: is, appear

Helping Verbs: are, will

Label the underlined verbs in the story below as *action, linking,* or *helping.* The first two have been done for you.

action *helping*

"Get down, Antonio. They will see you. Get down."

Everything was happening so fast. Captain Magellan was gone, the crew had scattered into the woods, and now we were under attack.

"Juan," whispered Antonio. "Since the captain is gone, you are now in charge. You must get us out of here."

Yes, Antonio was right. I, Juan Sebastian del Cano, was in charge. But get us out of here? How?

There was no chance that we would survive if we stayed on the ship. Escaping, as the crew had done, was our only hope.

"Antonio," I said, "we will swim for it."

Learning Language **Write the next part of the story. Underline and label the verbs: "A" for action, "L" for linking, or "H" for helping. Then tell a partner the end of the story using action, linking, and helping verbs.**

ELPS 2C, 4C, 5E

Simple Verb Tenses

Verb tenses tell the time of a verb. (See *Write Source* page 618.) The **present tense** of a verb describes something that is happening now or that happens regularly. The **past tense** of a verb describes something that happened in the past. The **future tense** of a verb describes something that will happen in the future.

Examples

Present Tense: The bear likes the sandwich.

Past Tense: The bear liked the sandwich.

Future Tense: The bear will like the sandwich.

Circle the present tense verb in each sentence below. Then, on the lines after each sentence, write the verb in the past tense and the future tense. The first sentence has been done for you.

	Past Tense	Future Tense
1. I (play) my stereo at top volume.	played	will play
2. I dance along to the music.		
3. No one likes the sound.		
4. The stereo blasts out music.		
5. My brother covers his ears.		
6. My mother rolls her eyes.		
7. My father laughs.		
8. Our dog Elvis howls.		
9. Our cat crawls under the chair.		

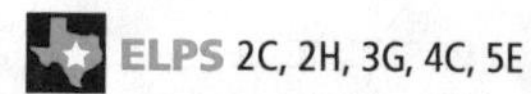

List three verbs below. (You can pick three from the list on page 622 of *Write Source*, or you can use any other verbs.) Then trade lists with a partner. For each of the three verbs you receive, write three sentences. Use the *present tense* of the verb in one sentence, the *past tense* in another sentence, and the *future tense* in your last sentence.

Three Verbs:

1. ____________________

2. ____________________

3. ____________________

Present Tense Sentences:

1. ____________________

2. ____________________

3. ____________________

Past Tense Sentences:

1. ____________________

2. ____________________

3. ____________________

Future Tense Sentences:

1. ____________________

2. ____________________

3. ____________________

Learning Language **Tell a partner three sentences about your past, your present, and your future. Use the correct verb tense for each situation.**

ELPS 4C

Singular and Plural Verbs 1

Use a **singular verb** when the subject in a sentence is singular. Use a **plural verb** when the subject is plural. (See *Write Source* page 620.)

Examples

Singular Verbs: talks, gives, clucks

Plural Verbs: talk, give, cluck

Directions

Give a name to each of the children below. Then write a sentence about each of them, using one of these singular verbs: *looks, wishes, waits, hopes, stares, listens, wonders, tries, keeps, sees, smiles*. The first one has been done for you.

____

1. *Marty stares at the hamster in the cage.*

Marty

2. ______________________________

3. ______________________________

____

____

4. ______________________________

5. ______________________________

____

ELPS 2C, 2H, 3G, 4C

Singular and Plural Verbs 2

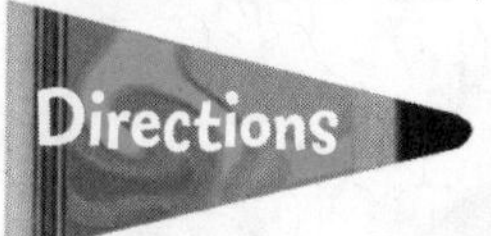

Directions **Check the verbs in the following sentences. If a verb is correct, underline it. If the verb is not correct, draw a line through it and write the correct form above it. The first one has been done for you.**

1. Wylan ~~kick~~ *kicks* the ball more than 30 yards.
2. These four boys run on the same relay team.
3. They practices twice a day.
4. Ms. Fry still coach the girls' softball team.
5. Is you happy about the color of the new uniforms?
6. The team's catcher want to buy a sandwich before the game.
7. Who waters the football field in the summer?
8. The gymnasts puts chalk on their hands.
9. Fifteen players runs laps every day.
10. Coach Fry show the team how to catch a fly ball.

Learning Language **Write three sentences with the word *children* as the subject. Use one of these plural verbs in each of your sentences: *wonder, hope,* and *see.* Then tell a partner two new sentences. Use a singular verb in one and a plural verb in the other.**

TEKS 4.20A(i)
ELPS 2C, 2H, 3G, 4C, 5E

Irregular Verbs 1

To make most verbs past tense, you simply add *-ed* to the end. Easy. But then there are **irregular verbs**. They're called irregular because you don't make them past tense in the regular way. (For a list of irregular verbs, see *Write Source* page 622.)

Examples

Irregular Verbs: ride, rode, ridden
run, ran, run
set, set, set

Study the chart of irregular verbs on *Write Source* page 622. Then close your book and fill in the missing words in the chart below.

present tense	past tense	past participle
1. break		*(have) broken*
2. bring		
3. come	*came*	
4. drink		*(have) drunk*
5. know	*knew*	
6. lead		
7. shake		*(have) shaken*
8. sing		*(have) sung*
9. speak	*spoke*	

Learning Language **Write three sentences that use past-tense irregular verbs. Then tell a partner two new sentences. In each sentence, use one of the irregular verbs on this page in the past participle.**

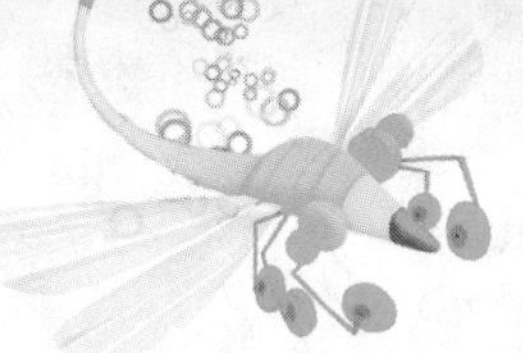

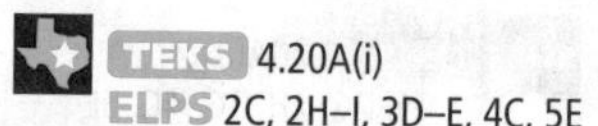

Irregular Verbs 2

This exercise gives you practice using **irregular verbs**. (Before you begin, review the chart of irregular verbs on *Write Source* page 622.)

Examples

Irregular Verbs:	see	saw	seen
	sit	sat	sat
	burst	burst	burst

In each sentence below, fill in the blank with the correct form of the verb that appears in parentheses. Try doing this without looking at your textbook. The first sentence has been done for you.

1. The rain ___froze___ and made the streets slick. *(freeze)*
2. Our cat's water was ______________ , too. *(freeze)*
3. My uncle ______________ me to a museum last week. *(take)*
4. He has ______________ me to a lot of fun places. *(take)*
5. I ______________ up at 7:00 a.m. yesterday. *(wake)*
6. I ______________ my bike to my cousin's house. *(ride)*
7. I had never ______________ there before. *(ride)*
8. Misha was ______________ by a spider. *(bite)*
9. The spider ______________ him on the foot. *(bite)*
10. His neighbor ______________ over to look at it. *(come)*

Learning Language **Write three sentences with past-tense irregular verbs. Then tell a partner a sentence with a present-tense irregular verb. Ask your partner to repeat the sentence back to you with the verb changed to past tense.**

TEKS 4.20A(i)
ELPS 4C, 5D

Irregular Verbs Review 1

This activity gives you more practice with irregular verbs.

To practice using irregular verbs, change the underlined verbs to the past tense. The first sentence has been done for you.

The doorbell ~~rings~~ rang. I wake up. It is Saturday morning, and the snow is coming down hard. My uncle stands outside our door with a huge package, taller than I am. He brings the package inside. A freezing wind blows in. With a wink and a smile, he says the present is for me. It isn't my birthday or anything. He sets it in the hallway. "Don't open it yet," he says. "What's for breakfast?" I eat in a hurry. My uncle drinks coffee and talks to my mom. I steal glances at the package. I fight the urge to run to the hallway and open it. Finally my uncle says, "Well, I guess it's time!" I run to the hallway. I shake the box—it is not heavy at all for such a big box. I lay it on its side. I tear off the wrapping paper. At the bottom of the box, something shines like silver . . . silver with a long wooden handle. It is a snow shovel! My uncle bursts out laughing. "Let it snow, let it snow, let it snow!" he sings. I begin to plan my revenge, but then my uncle makes it up to me: He takes me to the movies.

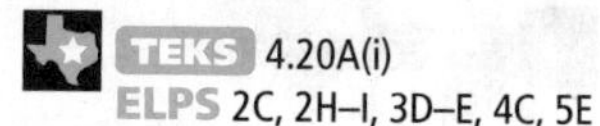

Irregular Verbs Review 2

Check the sentences below to make sure the irregular verbs are spelled correctly. Circle the correct ones. Cross out each incorrect verb and write the correct form above it.

1. Yesterday, Jane bited into an apple and breaked a tooth.
2. The cell phone rang five times before someone answered it.
3. Janis weared a new pair of shoes for the field trip.
4. The team swam 15 laps last Thursday.
5. Susan knowed the answer to the pop quiz question.
6. Bryan washed his new sweater in hot water, and it shrinked.
7. Wind blowed down the old elm tree on the corner.
8. Mrs. Johnston teached me how to weave on a floor loom.
9. Taking his time, Sam drew a beautiful picture of a parrot.
10. The class plant growed nine inches during the summer.
11. My mother freezed the juice and maked popsicles.
12. Billy said, " I seed five deer in the park."
13. On the class trip, Lori buyed a souvenir agate.

Learning Language **Write three sentences of your own using past-tense irregular verbs from this page. Tell a partner two new sentences with past-tense irregular verbs. Have your partner use the same verbs in two sentences in present tense.**

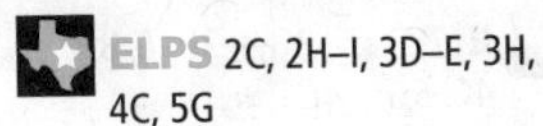
ELPS 2C, 2H–I, 3D–E, 3H, 4C, 5G

Adjectives

An **adjective** is a word that describes a noun or a pronoun. Adjectives can answer questions like *What kind?* or *How many?* Some adjectives describe the subject of a sentence but follow a linking verb. (See *Write Source* page 624.)

Examples

The huge garage sale was a fund-raising activity.

Twenty helpful people donated incredible items.

The crowd of noisy, eager buyers was larger than we expected.

Circle the adjectives in the sentences below. Each sentence contains at least three. Do not circle *a, an,* or *the*. The first sentence has been done for you.

1. One person gave us a red mixing bowl and six old umbrellas.
2. Miriam used two rags to clean a cardboard box of dusty books.
3. They were interesting, and a white-haired lady gave us a friendly smile when she bought them.
4. A new, unopened bottle of sweet perfume brought the best price.
5. A frying pan and a raggedy woollen coat, however, did not sell.
6. We also sold many tasty treats, such as chicken sandwiches, fresh lemonade, and hot apple dumplings.

Learning Language **Write five sentences about things that you might find at a garage sale. Use descriptive adjectives to tell about the items. Then use descriptive adjectives to tell a partner a few sentences about yourself. Have your partner identify the adjectives you used.**

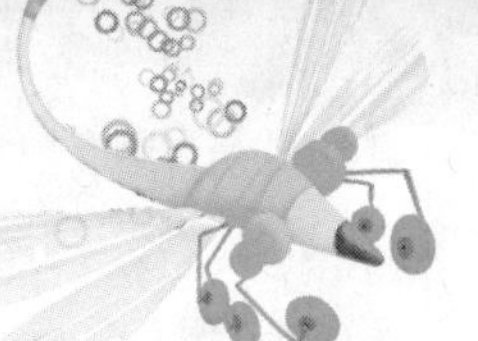

ELPS 2C, 2G–I, 3D–E, 3H, 4C, 5G

Common and Proper Adjectives

Proper adjectives are formed from proper nouns and are capitalized. All other adjectives are **common adjectives**. (See *Write Source* page 624.)

Example

The American continents are North America and South America.

Read the sentences below, checking that proper adjectives are capitalized and that common adjectives are not. Make the necessary changes. The first sentence has been done for you.

1. Of the ~~S~~seven continents, the ~~a~~Asian continent is the largest one.
2. The coldest continent is Antarctica.
3. The czech Republic is located on the european continent.
4. African animal herds are Larger than anywhere else.
5. The european and asian continents border each other in Russia.
6. Part of Antarctica, the ross Ice Shelf, is about the size of France.
7. Southern Asia has the world's Tallest peaks, in the himalayan Mountains.
8. The platypus and the kangaroo, which are australian animals, are two of the most Unusual creatures in the world.
9. The asian body of water called the dead Sea is one of the Saltiest places on the planet.

Learning Language **Write a short paragraph about your state using both common and proper adjectives. Then tell a partner a sentence about the street that you live on. Discuss which adjectives are proper.**

ELPS 2C, 2H, 3G, 4C

Demonstrative Adjectives

The **demonstrative adjectives**, *this, that, these,* and *those,* are used to point out specific nouns. *This* and *that* are used with singular nouns, while *these* and *those* are used with plural nouns. (See *Write Source* page 624.)

Underline the demonstrative adjectives in the following sentences. If they are not used correctly, change them. The first one has been done for you.

1. The cold snap froze these (this) bucket of water.
2. That plants lost their leaves because of the cold weather.
3. A gentle snowfall covered those steps overnight.
4. The cold air caused this bugs to hide under these woodpile.
5. These window has frost on it, but those window does not.
6. The temperature is 25 degrees according to this thermometer.
7. Is those thermometer Celsius or Fahrenheit?
8. These thermometer is Fahrenheit.
9. I didn't notice the frost on these spiderwebs yesterday.
10. That frost designs on the web are beautiful.

Learning Language **Write four sentences about crayons using the demonstrative adjectives *this, that, these,* and *those*. Then use demonstrative adjectives to tell a partner where objects are located around the classroom.**

Forms of Adjectives

The **positive form** of an adjective describes a noun without comparing it to anyone or anything else. The **comparative form** of an adjective compares two people, places, things, or ideas. The **superlative form** compares three or more people, places, things, or ideas. (See *Write Source* page 626.)

Examples

Positive: Miguel is a fast runner.

Comparative: He is faster than anyone else on the team.

Superlative: He is the fastest runner in the league.
(Use *-er* and *-est* for short adjectives.)

Positive: Sylvia is a skillful skateboarder.

Comparative: She is more skillful now than she was last year.

Superlative: She is now the most skillful skateboarder on her block.
(Use *more* and *most* with adjectives of two or more syllables.)

Directions **In the sentences below, write the correct form of the adjectives shown in parentheses.**

1. I learned that diamond is the _________ mineral on earth. *(hard)*
2. Manuel's new shirt is made of _________ cotton. *(soft)*
3. Jill says that roses are __________________ than daisies. *(beautiful)*
4. Frank is the _________ boy in his class and wants to play basketball. *(tall)*
5. Rubbing his hands together, Jon said, "It is really __________." *(cold)*
6. Sue's twisted ankle was _______________ today than yesterday. *(painful)*

Learning Language **Write three sentences about an activity you like to do. Use positive, comparative, and superlative adjectives. Then tell a partner two sentences about books or movies you like. Be sure to use a comparative and superlative adjectives.**

TEKS 4.20A(iv)
ELPS 2H, 3H, 4C, 5G

Adverbs

An **adverb** is a word that describes a verb, an adjective, or another adverb. Most adverbs answer *when, where,* or *how* questions. (See *Write Source* page 628.)

Example

Describing a Verb:

The kindergartners go **annually** to a farm.

In the following sentences about field trips, circle the adverbs and underline the verbs they describe. The first sentence has been done for you. *Hint:* Sometimes more than one adverb in the same sentence can describe the same word.

1. The first-grade class (always) <u>takes</u> a trip to the zoo (early) in the fall.
2. Sometimes the second-grade class visits a local farm to pick apples.
3. The third grade usually travels down to the natural history museum and then writes a class report about endangered species.
4. Surprisingly, the fourth grade often votes for a field day to clean up the vacant lots in the neighborhood.
5. The fifth-grade class happily goes away to science camp for three days in the spring.
6. The sixth graders proudly march in the Earth Day parade.

Learning Language **Write a short paragraph about a trip you have taken. Use adverbs to describe *where, when,* and *how*. Then tell a partner about a trip you would like to take. Use the adverbs *usually* and *a lot* to in your description.**

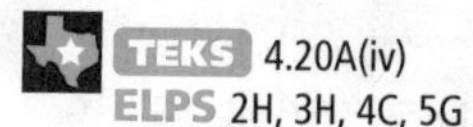

Types of Adverbs

Adverbs are used to modify verbs, adjectives, or other adverbs. Adverbs of time tell *when, how often,* or *how long* an action is done. Adverbs of place explain *where* something happens or *where* something is. Adverbs of manner say *how* something is done. Adverbs of degree show *how much* or *how little*. (See *Write Source* page 628.)

Examples

Time: Jim crossed the street **last**. *(when)*

Place: He crossed the street **there**. *(where)*

Manner: He crossed the street **quickly**. *(how)*

Degree: He crossed the street **very** quickly. *(how much)*

Complete the sentences using the listed adverbs. The type of adverb to use for each sentence is given. The first one has been done for you.

scarcely	inside	down	quickly
always	very	twice	cheerfully

1. On rainy days, Orin walks ___quickly___ to school. *(manner)*
2. Even with an umbrella, he still gets ____________ wet. *(degree)*
3. If the rainfall is heavy, he waits ____________. *(place)*
4. Orin has been soaked ____________ this month. *(time)*
5. He ____________ keeps a dry change of clothes in his locker. *(time)*
6. Water from his wet clothes drips ____________ on the floor. *(place)*
7. Orin is ____________ bothered by the rain even if he gets wet. *(degree)*
8. He ____________ says that we are 60 percent water anyway. *(manner)*

Learning Language **Write a few sentences describing what you do on a rainy day. Use at least two adverbs from the list on this page. Then tell a partner about how you get to school. Use adverbs to describe *when, where, how,* and *how much*.**

TEKS 4.20A(iv)
ELPS 2C, 4C

Forms of Adverbs

There are three forms of adverbs: the **positive** form, the **comparative** form, and the **superlative** form. (See page 630 in *Write Source*. Make sure to note the irregular forms for *well* and *badly*.)

Examples

Positive:
I run swiftly and jump high.

Comparative:
He runs more swiftly and jumps higher.

Superlative:
She runs most swiftly and jumps highest.

In each sentence, fill in the blanks with the correct forms of the adverb in boldface. The first sentence has been done for you.

1. Zoe did **well** on the test, but Jolene did ____better____, and Bianca did the ____best____.

2. Jerry talks **fast,** but Yolanda talks ____________, and Laurie talks the ____________.

3. We did **badly** in the race, but Mike's team did ____________, and Georgia's team did the ____________.

4. Rolly swims **well,** but Lamar swims ____________, and Felix swims ____________ of them all.

5. Angela climbed **carefully,** but Gary climbed ____________, and Eric climbed ____________ to the top of the climbing wall.

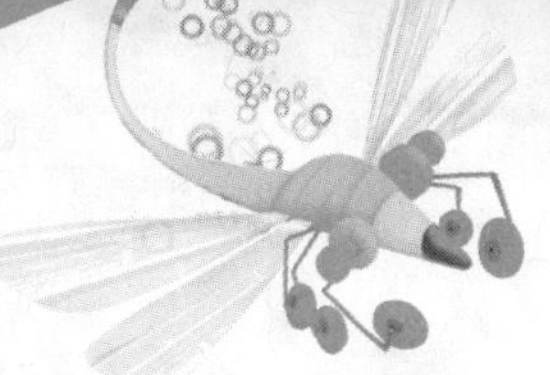

6. John studies **hard,** but Sharon studies ______________, and Tomas studies ______________ of all.

7. Joanne speaks **clearly,** but Fumiko speaks ______________, and Sam speaks ______________ during speeches.

8. Paloma sings **beautifully,** but Elena sings ______________, and Susan sings ______________.

Directions Fill in the comparative and superlative forms of the following adverbs. Then write sentences using all three forms of each adverb. (See *Write Source* page 630 for help.)

Positive Form	Comparative Form	Superlative Form
badly		
bravely		
late		
well		

1. (badly) ______________________________

____

2. (bravely) ______________________________

____

3. (late) ______________________________

____

Learning Language Use comparative and superlative forms of the adverb *well* to tell a partner about something you can do.

4.20A(v)
ELPS 2C, 4C

Prepositional Phrases 1

A **prepositional phrase** gives details about other words in a sentence. It starts with a **preposition,** and it includes an object and usually one or more modifying words. A preposition never appears by itself. (See *Write Source* page 632.)

Example

Take a Walk in Their Shoes is a great book!
(The word *in* is a preposition; the words *in Their Shoes* is a prepositional phrase.)

Each book title below has one preposition. Circle each preposition. Underline the entire prepositional phrase. The first one has been done for you.

1. *About the B'Nai Bagels*
2. *Among the Volcanoes*
3. *A Blessing in Disguise*
4. *Boys at Work*
5. *Bridge to Terabithia*
6. *The Summer of the Swans*
7. *Journey into Terror*
8. *Little House on the Prairie*
9. *Sees Behind Trees*
10. *In the Language of Loons*
11. *Sybil Rides for Independence*
12. *Diary of a Drummer Boy*
13. *A Letter to Amy*
14. *When I Was Young in the Mountains*
15. *Song of the Trees*
16. *Arthur for the Very First Time*
17. *On the Riverbank*
18. *Sweet Rhymes Around the World*
19. *Sideways Stories from Wayside School*
20. *If You Grew Up with George Washington*

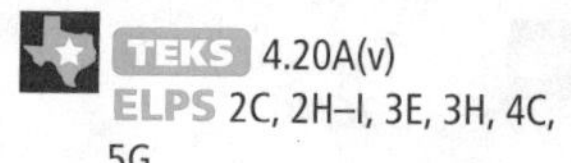

Prepositional Phrases 2

In the paragraph below, underline all the prepositions and double underline the rest of the prepositional phrase. The first one has been done for you.

Jake noticed that new tires eventually wear thin. His father told him that the tires get worn away by the road. Jake knew that there are millions of cars wearing their tires out all the time. He wondered why he didn't see huge piles of tire tread along the highways. Where did all of that rubber go? So Jake went to the library, and he read articles on the Internet. He discovered that carmakers and others had asked this same question. They were worried that flying tire tread might be harmful to people's health. Jake learned that the tread breaks into tiny pieces. Wind, rain, and sun help break down those little pieces even more. Very little of the tire tread stays in the air. Even the rubber dust in the air doesn't stay there long. The tiny pieces of tire tread blow away or become part of the ground. Jake told his father about his special studies. His father was impressed.

Learning Language **Use prepositions to write a detailed description of where you sit in your classroom. Then describe the location of an object in your classroom to a partner. Use as many prepositional phrases as you can. See if your partner can figure out the object you selected.**

 ELPS 2C, 4C

Coordinating Conjunctions

A **coordinating conjunction** connects equal parts of a sentence: two or more words, two or more phrases, or two or more clauses. The coordinating conjunctions are *and, but, or, nor, for, so,* and *yet.* (See *Write Source* page 634.)

Examples

Connecting Words: Mugs and Barney barked.

Connecting Phrases: Kat ran out the door and into the yard.

Connecting Clauses: Kat kept running, and Mugs followed.

Directions **Circle all the coordinating conjunctions in the following paragraph.**

When I was little, I was scared of the dark. I thought monsters or ghosts would come out and yell, "Boo!" I imagined closets hiding goblins or wild animals. Finally, I got a night-light, and it worked like a charm. It was shaped like a seashell, and I could see its friendly glow in the dark. It lit up my room a little, so I could sleep better. Through the years, I enjoyed having my night-light right next to my bed. Now I am older, and I don't need it anymore.

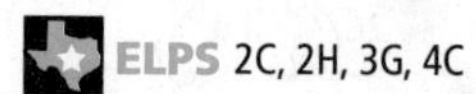

On the center of the lines below, copy some of the coordinating conjunctions you circled. On either side, write the words, phrases, or clauses that each conjunction connects. Two have been done for you.

1. ____________________

2. ____________________

3. *I got a night-light,* *and* *it worked like a charm.*

4. *It lit up my room a little,* *so* *I could sleep better.*

5. ____________________

Learning Language **Choose another student model from your textbook or something from your own writing folder. Find five phrases or clauses that contain coordinating conjunctions and write them here. Then tell a partner two new sentences using coordinating conjunctions.**

1. ____________________

2. ____________________

3. ____________________

4. ____________________

5. ____________________

ELPS 2C, 4C

Subordinating Conjunctions

A **subordinating conjunction** connects two clauses to make a complex sentence. The subordinating conjunction may come at the beginning or in the middle of the sentence. (See *Write Source* page 634.)

Examples

After we went to the game, we stopped for ice cream.

We stopped for ice cream after we went to the game.

Circle the subordinating conjunction in each sentence below. The first one has been done for you.

1. (Because) I missed the bus, I was late for school.
2. We play soccer in this park after school lets out.
3. We'll have to go inside if we see lightning.
4. We can't go swimming until the rain stops.
5. I won't finish my homework unless I start soon.
6. While I clean our room, Polly will walk the dog.
7. When I finish my homework, I'll call Sam.
8. Juanita couldn't come to school because she was sick.
9. Since it is dark, I don't want to walk home alone.
10. I like my aunt because she is funny.
11. Before we moved, I went to a different school.

From the previous exercise, choose three sentences that begin with subordinating conjunctions. Write them with the conjunction in the middle.

Examples

Because I missed the bus, I was late for school.

I was late for school because I missed the bus.

1. ______________________________

____

2. ______________________________

____

3. ______________________________

____

Directions

Choose three sentences with subordinating conjunctions in the middle. Rewrite each sentence so the subordinating conjunction is at the beginning.

1. ______________________________

____

2. ______________________________

____

3. ______________________________

____

Learning Language **Tell a partner a sentence about your trip to school this morning. Use at least one sentence that begins with a subordinating conjunction and one sentence that has a subordinating conjunction in the middle.**

TEKS 4.20A(vii)
ELPS 2C, 3D, 4C

Correlative Conjunctions

Correlative conjunctions work together as pairs to connect two similar subjects or ideas. The correlative conjunction pairs are: *either/or, neither/nor, not only/but also, both/and, whether/or* and *as/so*. (See *Write Source* page 634.)

Examples

Connecting Subjects:
Both my parents and I want to go to the Texas Folklife Festival.

Connecting Ideas:
Whether we go on Saturday or we go on Sunday, we'll have a good time.

Directions

Circle the correlative conjunctions in the following paragraphs. Remember: They come in pairs. The first pair has been marked for you.

The cultural groups at the festival (both) celebrate (and) share their traditions. One of my parents bought tickets either online or at the supermarket. Whether Mom or Dad paid for them, I was glad to have them. Then off we went!

The program we got not only listed activities but also had a helpful map. Neither my parents nor I could decide what to do first. After all, both the Cajun band and the Chinese dancers looked like fun. By the end of the day, not only had we seen them and other groups perform, but we also had learned about many cultures.

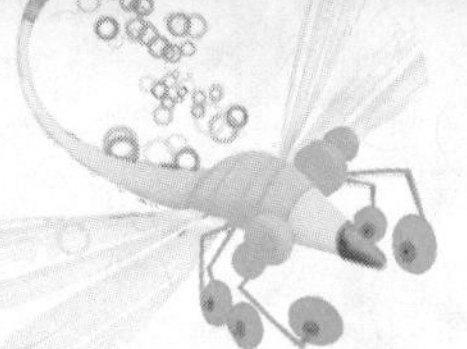

From the previous exercise, choose three sentences that have correlative conjunctions. Rewrite each sentence to change the words that the conjunctions connect.

Examples

The groups at the festival **both** celebrate **and** share their traditions.

The groups at the festival **both** display crafts **and** answer questions.

1. ______________________________

____

2. ______________________________

____

3. ______________________________

____

Learning Language **Choose three sentences from your text or a piece from your own writing folder. Rewrite each sentence to use correlative conjunctions. Change other words as needed. Compare the conjunctions that you used with a partner. Then tell your partner a new sentence using a different pair of correlative conjunctions.**

1. ______________________________

____

2. ______________________________

____

3. ______________________________

____

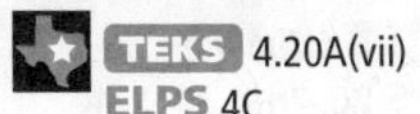
TEKS 4.20A(vii)
ELPS 4C

Conjunctions Review

This activity is a review of the three types of conjunctions.

Each sentence has either a coordinating conjunction, a subordinating conjunction, or correlative conjunctions. Underline the conjunctions. Write "C" above coordinating conjunctions, "S" above subordinating conjunctions, and "CR" above correlative conjunctions. The first sentence has been done.

1. My sister and (C) I washed our dog after (S) he rolled in the mud.
2. We will play both basketball and soccer.
3. Jerry has to change clothes and clean his room before he can play.
4. We went to the mall, yet we couldn't find the store where we had seen the video game.
5. Though it was almost time for dinner, we ate grapes and cheese.
6. We're not hungry, but we'll eat if you're having pizza!
7. Stephanie and I walked to the museum after we rode the bus downtown.
8. Jim or Amir can feed the fish while Sandy waters the plants.
9. I can either watch TV, or I can finish my homework.
10. Because it's raining, my mom or dad will pick me up.
11. Although Heather had a cat, she still wanted a parakeet and a lovebird.
12. Speeding in a car is not only illegal, but also dangerous.

Directions **Add the needed conjunctions to the sentences below.**

1. __________ it's 9:00, Lilly __________ James are still sleeping.
2. It's Tuesday, __________ practice is canceled __________ it's raining.
3. My dad honked the horn, __________ the cow stayed in the road __________ another car came along.
4. __________ the boots seemed big enough, John could not get them on his feet.
5. Sue laughed out loud __________ rolling in the snow.
6. Mom __________ Dad will make some hot chocolate __________ the sledding party.
7. Luann didn't feel well, __________ she drank some tea __________ took a nap.
8. We will go to the shore __________ it rains __________ it is sunny.
9. __________ John __________ Maria can go to the movies tonight.

Learning Language **Use coordinating, subordinating, and correlative conjunctions to write a paragraph about what you plan to do this weekend. Circle and identify each conjunction you use. Then tell a partner a new sentence that uses a correlative conjunction. Have your partner identify the correlative conjunction pair that you used.**

4.20A(viii)
ELPS 2H, 3G, 4C, 5F–G

Transitions 1

A **transition** is a word or phrase that helps to connect ideas in one sentence or paragraph to another. For example, the transitions *before, then,* and *as soon as* show time-order connections. (See *Write Source* pages 519–520 for a list of other transitions.)

Example

Kim finished her art homework **before** her family ate dinner.

As soon as everyone finished eating, she practiced piano and **then** watched some TV.

Complete the following paragraph by adding transitions that show time order. Choose from the list of transitions below. For each blank, write the transition that makes the most sense. Use each transition just once. The first one has been done for you.

after   as soon as   before   during   finally   next   soon   then

We had a terrific pizza dinner. __Before__ we turned on the oven, we made the crust and __________ set out the ingredients. __________ that was done, we spread tomato sauce on the crust. __________, we sprinkled spices and cheese over the sauce. We put the pizza in the oven __________ we added mushrooms to it. __________ a delicious smell filled the house. __________ that time, we set the table. The pizza came out of the oven, and we __________ sat down to a great meal!

Learning Language **Use time-order transitions to write four or five sentences that tell a story. Then tell your partner what you did last weekend using time-order transition words.**

Transitions 2

Transitions are "connecting" words and phrases. They show how those ideas are related. For example, some transitions show a summary or a conclusion. (See *Write Source* pages 519–520.)

Example

A rainstorm suddenly blew in. As a result, our picnic came to an end.

Choose from the list below to add a summary or conclusion transition to each of the following sentences or sentence pairs. The first one has been done for you.

as a result, because finally, in conclusion, lastly, meanwhile, on the other hand, therefore,

1. Jillian won first place in the school spelling bee. *Therefore,* she would go on to the city-wide contest.

2. The war was over. ____________ we could live our lives in peace.

3. The party was a success ____________ everyone cooperated and worked hard.

4. Thomas Edison invented a practical light bulb. ____________ people's lives changed in a dramatic way.

5. Thank you for listening to me today. And, ____________ remember what you have heard.

Learning Language **Write a sentence pair that shows a summary or conclusion. Use an appropriate transition to connect them. Then use a summary or conclusion transition to tell a partner the ending to a speech you would like to give.**

ELPS 2C, 2H–I, 3D–E, 4C

Interjections

An **interjection** is a word or phrase used to express surprise or strong emotion. A comma or an exclamation point sets off an interjection from the rest of the sentence. (See *Write Source* page 636.)

Examples

Yikes! The cat's in the top tree branches!

Did you hear that motorcycle? Wow!

Watch where you're going, hey!

Man, that's dangerous!

Fill in the blanks in the paragraph below with interjections from the list. The first one has been done for you.

Boy	Well	Good point	Wait	Oh no
Help	Wrong	My goodness	Wow	Yikes

Do you know that the world's fastest plane can fly 2,000 miles per hour? ___Wow___! I could fly across the country in an hour and a half. If I didn't want to fly, how fast could I go? __________, the world's fastest train in Japan can reach 190 miles per hour. __________________! Everything outside the windows would look blurry. I bet cars can't go that fast. __________! A company in Germany can change a regular sports car so it can reach 210 miles per hour. __________, we can't drive that fast.

Learning Language **Make up something silly and surprising to tell your partner. (For example: My little brother can walk on the ceiling.) Ask your partner to respond using an interjection.**

Parts of Speech Review 1

This activity is a review of all the parts of speech you have studied. Do the activity with a partner if your teacher allows it.

Each list below contains words that are examples of one part of speech. Label each list with the name of the correct part of speech.

1. ______	4. ______	7. ______
dog	run	I
book	said	you
California	throw	their
idea	write	his
mechanic	were	anyone

2. ______	5. ______	8. ______
quickly	big	of
loudly	tall	at
well	tallest	to
carefully	smart	over
down	an	on top of

3. ______	6. ______	9. ______
and	Hey!	as a result
or	Oh!	because
but	Wow!	meanwhile
because	Yikes!	after
although	Yes!	as soon as

Parts of Speech Review 2

This activity is a review of the parts of speech you have studied.

Read the following fable. Above each underlined word, write the correct part of speech. The first two have been done for you.

The Ant and the Dove

noun *verb*

One day, an ant crawled to a little pond to have a drink. When he was almost to the pond's edge, he fell down the slippery bank into the water. The ant was about to drown when a dove saw him. The dove quickly picked up a leaf and dropped it into the pond. The ant climbed onto the leaf and drifted safely back to land. As he stepped off the leaf, the ant looked up and saw a hunter who was taking aim at the dove with his gun. The tiny ant scurried up the hunter's boot and bit the hunter hard on the leg. The hunter yelled, "Ouch!" When the dove heard him, it flew away. The moral of the story is "One good turn deserves another."

Parts of Speech Review 3

This activity reviews the parts of speech you have studied.

Read the following paragraph. Write the underlined words in the correct columns below.

I recently saw an old picture of a suburb of Milwaukee, Wisconsin. Because the photo was 100 years old, it was black and white. Where tall pine trees once proudly stood, huge electrical towers now stretch their metal branches to the sky. Once a simple dirt path lead through the trees, but it has expanded into four-lane roads and broad concrete sidewalks. Wow! A quiet rural area turned into a very busy city.

Nouns	Verbs	Pronouns
____________	____________	____________
____________	____________	____________
____________	____________	____________
____________	____________	

Adverbs	Adjectives	Prepositions
____________	____________	____________
____________	____________	____________
____________	____________	____________

Interjections	Conjunctions	
____________	____________	____________
	____________	____________